THE CAMPAIGN IN ALSACE AUGUST 1870

Brigadier-General J.P. Du Cane, C.B.

Helion & Company Ltd

Helion & Company Limited
Unit 8 Amherst Business Centre
Budbrooke Road
Warwick
CV34 5WE
England
Tel. 01926 499619
Email: info@helion.co.uk
Website: www.helion.co.uk
X (formerly Twitter): @Helionbooks
Facebook: @HelionBooks
Visit our blog at https://helionbooks.wordpress.com/

Published by Helion & Company 2010. This new edition 2025
Originally published by Hugh Rees Ltd, London, 1912
Designed and typeset by Farr out Publications, Wokingham, Berkshire
Cover designed by Paul Hewitt, Battlefield Design (www.battlefield-design.co.uk)

ISBN 978-1-804518-82-3

British Library Cataloguing-in-Publication Data.
A catalogue record for this book is available from the British Library.

Contents

List of maps

Preface

This little book has been compiled from notes of lectures given at the Staff College in 1907, and has already appeared in the form of articles in the *Army Review.* The Comments have been brought up to date by the light of the Field Service Regulations and Training Manuals, which have appeared since the lectures were given.

The author has been tempted to publish these notes by the knowledge that many officers have a difficulty in applying the teaching of the official manuals, and that consequently there exists a demand for literature, which is explanatory of the views of the General Staff.

He does not suggest that his own opinions have any official sanction, and his object will be fulfilled if others, who are better qualified than himself to expound the official text-books, are encouraged to follow his example.

He has relied for his facts and for many of his Comments on the following works: – *French Official History, German Official History,* Bonnal's *Froeschweiler,* Henderson's *The Battle of Woerth.*[1]

His thanks are due to Capt. J. H. Davidson, King's Royal Rifles, for so kindly undertaking the work of preparing the maps, which were reproduced by the General Staff, War Office, and the Ordnance Survey, Southampton, and are published by permission of the Controller of HM Stationery Office.

1 Publisher's note – The works referred to are as follows: France, Army, État Major, Section Historique, *La Guerre de 1870/1,* publiée par la *Revue d'Histoire,* rédigée à la Section historique de l'État-Major de l'Armée (Paris, 1901-13, 22 vols); Germany, Army, Generalstab, Kriegsgeschichtliche Abteilung, *Der deutsch-französische Krieg 1870-1871,* 5 vols); Bonnal, G.A., *Froeschwiller: récit commenté des événements militaires, qui ont eu pour théatre le Palatinat bavarois, la basse Alsace et les Vosges moyennes du 15 Juillet en 12 Août 1870* (Paris, 1899, 2 vols incl atlas); Henderson, G.F.R., *The Battle of Wörth, August 6th 1870* (Yorktown, Surrey, 1899).

Introduction

A story is told of Lord Seaton, better known as Colonel Colbourne of Peninsular fame, that when asked how a man could best become proficient in the art of war he replied: "By fighting, Sir, and a great deal of it." By which no doubt that distinguished officer meant to imply that a little practice is worth a great deal of theory.

On the other hand, Frederick the Great's mule, which, in spite of its twenty campaigns, was "still a mule," is even more notorious. It lacked the brain power to apply its unique experience of war.

Given the brain power, no one would be so rash as to belittle the value of war experience. But the civilized world in the twentieth century is normally at peace, and if the officers of the armies of the great nations are to prepare themselves for war, some substitute must be found for actual war experience. We have, of course, a very excellent system of practical training with troops, but it is generally admitted that this system must be supplemented by study.

On this subject of study a well-known authority has written: "It is not pretended that study will make a dull man brilliant, nor confer resolution and rapid decision on one who is timid and irresolute by nature; but the quick, the resolute, the daring, deciding and acting rapidly, as is their nature, will be all the more likely to decide and act correctly in proportion as they have studied the art they are called upon to practice."

If study we should, it is obvious that we must turn to military history. But we may read military history with different objects in view namely, to study strategy and the higher branches of the art of war, or to extract from our reading tactical principles and to learn to apply them to the changed conditions of our own time.

As regards the first of these objects it is sometimes argued that such study is only necessary for officers who aspire to high command or to hold important positions on the staff. Colonel Henderson's opinion on this question is instructive. He held such views in the greatest contempt, going so far as to say that "this extraordinary doctrine is either an impudent excuse for idleness, or an abject admission that the more intellectual branch of the military art is utterly beyond the capacity of the ordinary officer."

If we are to accept this view of the necessity for the study of strategy – which is obviously the official view as officers are examined in the subject for promotion – what are we to say of the study of tactics? Surely that it is of greater importance still to all officers, who, to quote Henderson again, "aspire by any conceivable stretch of courtesy to be rightly called professional soldiers."

But when we come to consider how tactics are to be studied from history, we are confronted by a considerable difficulty. Whatever may be said of the immutability of the principles of strategy, there can be no question that the constant improvement of weapons affects tactics profoundly. Moreover, it takes time to write history. Before an account is published of the minor incidents of the battles of a great campaign, sufficiently detailed to enable us to study the tactical methods employed, the weapons that were used are out of date, and it has already become necessary to consider modifications in the application of tactical principles. As instances may be quoted the French Official History of the 1870 war, and the present state of our knowledge of the incidents of the Manchurian war. The former, for a variety of reasons, only began to appear about eight years ago, and it must be admitted that the light that has as yet been thrown on the minor tactics of Manchuria is imperfect.

How then is this difficulty to be surmounted? Henderson again comes to the rescue. When discussing tactical theory in the introduction to his pamphlet on the battle of Woerth he writes: "Theory is of two kinds. First, there is speculative theory, which, in default of great campaigns fought with modern matériel, endeavours, from a study of ballistics, of new inventions, of results on the ranges, of the incidents of manœuvres and field-days, to forecast the fighting of the future. Second, there is theory, which is based on the actual experience of war; theory, which does not neglect to consider the modifications which new arms and appliances may produce, but puts in the foreground the conditions which ruled the last great battles between civilized armies."

This view of the question is of considerable assistance in helping us over the stile. Theory, based on actual experience of war, must obviously rest on the lessons of military history. Speculative theory must be based on technical knowledge of the capacity of weapons and the imagination. The intelligent student of history will be able to discriminate between what he can accept as applicable to the present day and what he must discard as inapplicable, if he keeps this distinction in mind. But when he enters the realm of speculation, and history becomes an unreliable guide, to what is he to turn? The answer is supplied to us in some remarks of Colonel Gough in an article in a recent number of the Army Review. In dealing with the question of instruction in the application of tactical principles, he says that first class instructors are required who are fully conversant with the views of the General Staff.

Speculative theory must be supplied to the student by the General Staff, which, as a body, studies the lessons of history, picks the brains of the experts in weapons, and, combining judiciously the different aspects of these problems, builds up for us our theory of modern tactics, and embodies the result in our Field Service Regulations and Training Manuals. For the study of tactics from history to be profitable, therefore, it must be combined with the study of the Regulations published by the General Staff.

The primary object of this work is to illustrate the above arguments by an analysis of the tactical lessons of the battles of Weissenburg and Woerth, in order to show how abiding is the value of some of those lessons, and how necessary it is to modify some of the methods that were employed with success on those occasions. The references to the strategy of the campaign in Alsace are, therefore, limited to what is necessary to enable the reader to grasp the circumstances in which the battles were fought, and consequently to realize the necessity for adapting tactical dispositions to the strategical situation.

It is the author's hope that the method of analysis of the various incidents that has been adopted may be of some small assistance to officers who are compelled to study tactics from history without the aid of an instructor, and that they may be able to apply it with profit on their own account to other cases.

Chapter I

Weissenburg

Few battles bring out more clearly than Weissenburg the necessity to adapt tactical dispositions to the strategical situation. The 2nd Division of the Ist Corps (French), commanded by General Abel Douay, found itself at Weissenburg on the morning of the 4th August, 1870, within striking distance of greatly superior forces of the enemy. Its commander was imperfectly informed as to the situation and was without clear instructions as to how he should act if attacked. The Division was surprised in its bivouac, attacked by overwhelming forces and defeated with heavy losses. It is necessary to understand how these events came about in order to appreciate fully the tactical lessons of the battle.

German concentration and plan of Campaign

Moltke's plan of campaign was based on the assumption that the French would assemble their army on the line Strasburg-Metz and "avoiding our strong front on the Rhine, push forward to the Main, separate North from South Germany, come to terms with the latter, and use that country as a base for further offensive operations on the Elbe."[1] To counteract such a plan and at the same time prepare for an offensive at the earliest possible moment in the greatest possible strength in the most effective direction, it was decided to concentrate the whole of the available German forces in the Bavarian Palatinate on both banks of the Rhine.

If the French were to concentrate considerable forces in Alsace, and, seizing the initiative, were to threaten South Germany by crossing the Upper Rhine; the German left wing could advance up the left bank of the Rhine and paralyse the French offensive. South Germany would thus be indirectly protected.

If, on the other hand, the German mobilization were to prove the more rapid of the two, as there was every reason to expect, the bulk of the German Army could cross the Saar and enter Lorraine with superior forces, which movement, being on the direct road to Paris, could be confidently expected to throw the French on the defensive in the main theatre.

In order to carry out this plan it was decided to assemble the troops in three armies:

- The Ist Army (about 60,000 men) near Wittlich to form the right wing.
- The IInd Army (about 130,000 men) in the area Neurkirchen-Homburg to form the centre.
- The IIIrd Army (about 130,000 men) about Landau and Rastatt to form the left wing.

It is with the IIIrd Army only that we are concerned. That army consisted of the Vth and XIth Prussian Corps, the Bavarians, Wurtembergers and Badeners.

The bulk of the troops concentrated behind the Klingbach, covered by the 4th Bavarian Division at Bergzabern and the 42nd Brigade of the XIth Corps at Langenkandel.

The distribution of the troops in the area of concentration was as follows, see Map I:

1 *German Official History.*

THE FRANCO-GERMAN FRONTIER

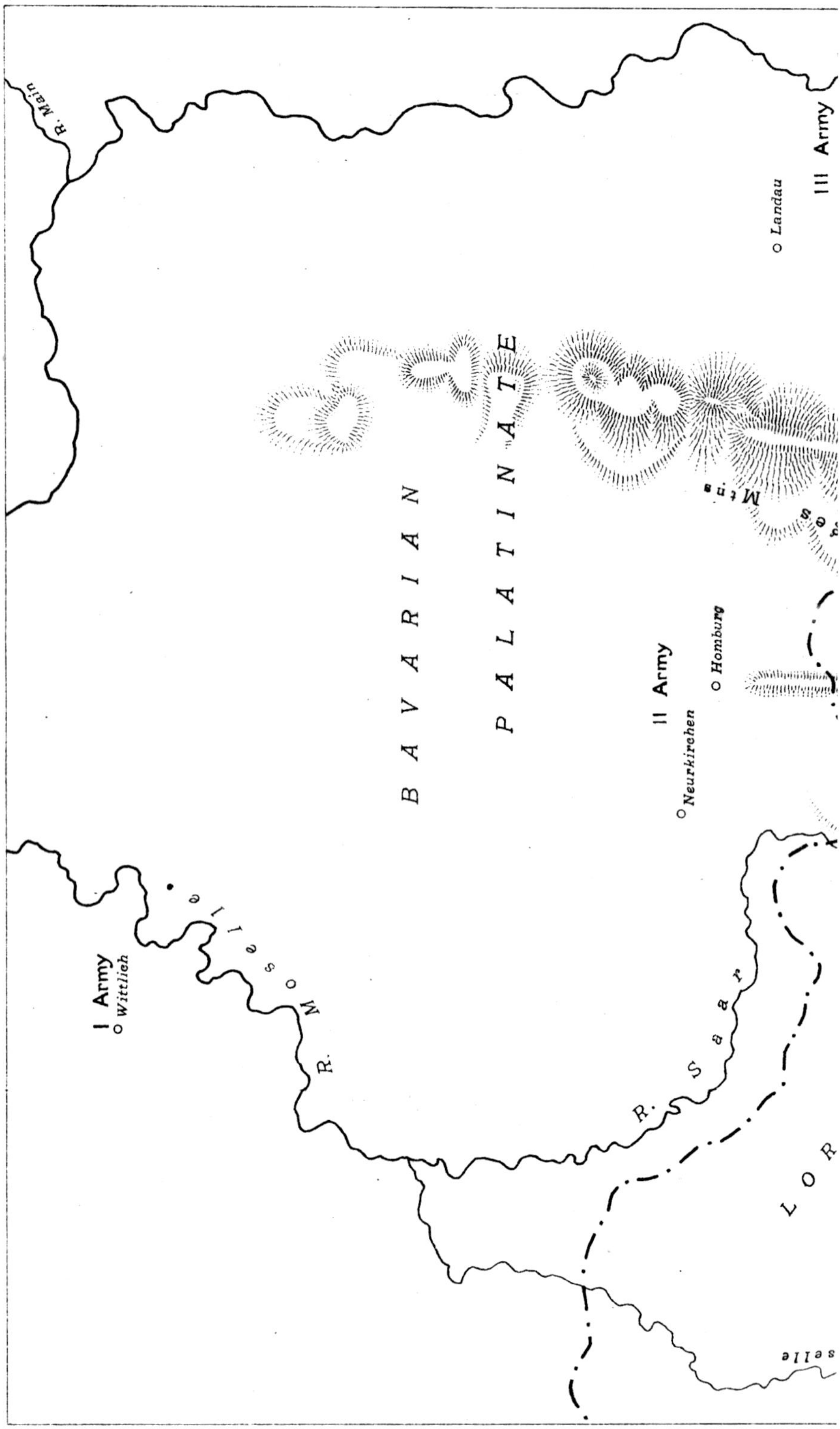

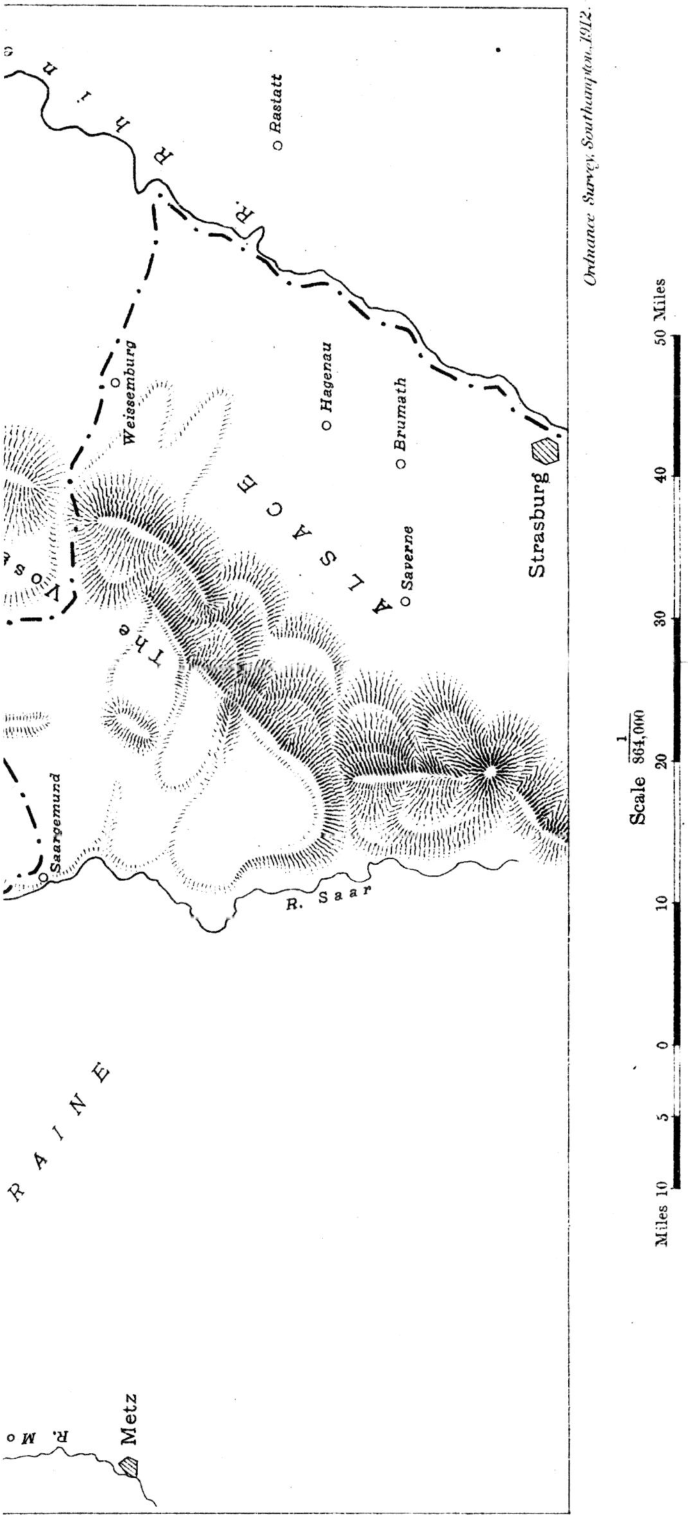
Ordnance Survey, Southampton, 1912.
Rastatt
Weissemburg
Hagenau
Brumath
Strasburg
ALSACE
Saverne
The
Saargemund
R. Saar
Metz
Scale 1/864,000
Miles 10 5 0 10 20 30 40 50 Miles

Map I

Vth Corps and 4th Cavalry Division round Landau.
XIth Corps round Germersheim.
Ist Bavarian Corps round Speyer.
IInd Bavarian Corps round Neustadt.
Werder's Corps { (Baden Division) Karlsruhe.
{(Wurtemburg Divin.), Graben.

The covering troops pushed forward detachments to the line Pfortz-Schaidt-Steinfeld-Kapsweyer-Schweigen and thence to Pirmasens. Some insignificant cavalry reconnaissances were carried out across the frontier, but gleaned little information of value. The mobilization and concentration of the 4th Cavalry Division were seriously delayed and the division was not formed till 1st August.

Such was the situation at the beginning of 1 August when it was known at the German Head Quarters that the French were assembling a considerable part of their army in Alsace. Moltke then allotted an independent mission to the IIIrd Army, namely, to seek out and destroy the French forces in Alsace. Should the French be defeated and driven back on Strasburg the Crown Prince was ordered to watch and contain them with a portion of his force, while moving the bulk of his troops North across the Vosges, so as to be in a position to operate against the right flank of the main French Army in Lorraine. Should the French cross the Vosges without awaiting attack the IIIrd Army was ordered to move along the Palatinate frontier towards the Saar, so as to reach the neighbourhood of Saargemund on the 9th August.

It was important, therefore, that the IIIrd Army should advance on the earliest possible date. Accordingly, the Crown Prince, on the urgent representations of Moltke, conveyed to him personally by Colonel von Verdy, ordered the army to be prepared to advance on the 4th August without its trains, which were net yet complete, and as a preparatory measure the Corps were ordered to close up and concentrate in bivouac as follows on the 3rd[2]:-

4th Bavarian Division – Bergzabern. Advanced Guard to the Army.
Vth Corps, Billigheim.
XIth Corps, Rohrbach.
Remainder of IInd Bavarian Corps, Walsheim (north of Landau).
Ist Bavarian Corps, west of Germersheim.
Werder's Corps { (Badeners, Pfortz.
{ (Wurtemburgers, Knielingen.
4th Cavalry Division. Offenbach (east of Landau).

It will be seen, therefore, that the IIIrd Army was assembled with one Division as advanced guard, 3 corps in front line and 1½ corps in second line, but, unfortunately, the Cavalry Division was still in rear.

A few comments only are necessary on these dispositions.

The concentration was screened by the Bienwald and the Klingbach, a judicious arrangement which would have made it difficult for French reconnoitring detachments to obtain definite information had such been employed. On the other hand, the open country between the Vosges and the Bienwald in the neighbourhood of the frontier is restricted. It was, therefore, very desirable to ensure the passage of the Lauter and the exits from the Bienwald without risk of attack by the enemy. This pointed to the urgent necessity for accurate information as to the position of the enemy's main forces in Alsace

2 See Map II.

ORIGINAL CONCENTRATION OF GERMAN III ARMY

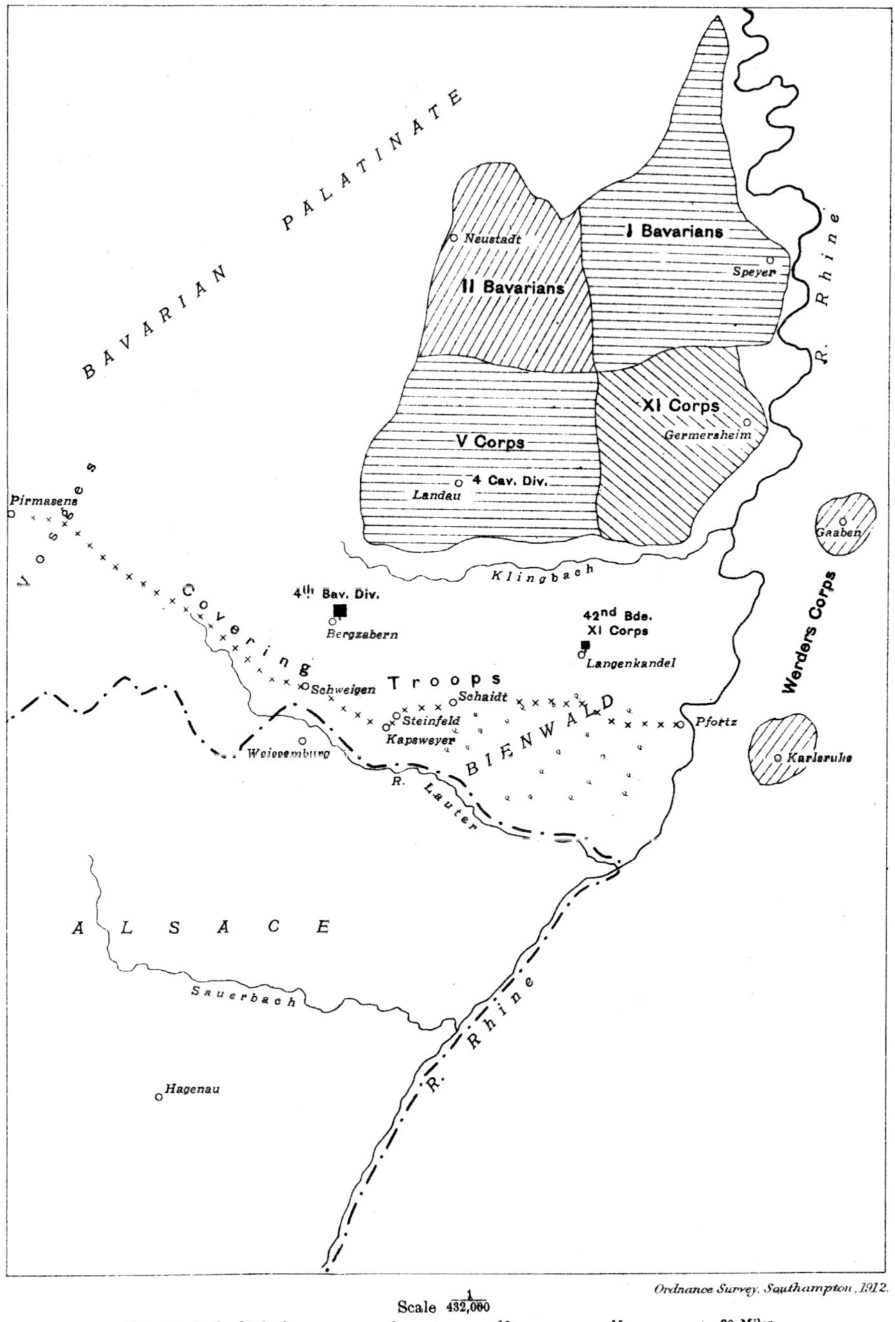

Map II

before the advance took place, and emphasized the evil effects of the tardy mobilization of the 4th Cavalry Division. If that division had crossed the Lauter either on the 3rd August, or even early on the 4th, and had pushed reconnaissances to the south towards the Sauer, much useful information would have been obtained and the state of uncertainty that existed after a successful action would have been avoided.

It is curious that the Crown Prince should have considered it necessary to assemble the various corps of his army in bivouac, each in a very limited space on the 3rd August, before advancing. To concentrate to such an extent hardly seems to have been desirable, as the troops must necessarily open out again on the following day when they advanced. Some closing up of the billeting areas was advisable, but the principle of billeting in depth, along the road by which it is intended to advance, was certainly applicable to the situation.

The following is a summary of the Crown Prince's orders for the 4th August, as given in the German Official History:

> It is my intention tomorrow to advance with the army as far as the Lauter and to throw vanguards across it. With this object the Bienwald will be traversed on four roads. The enemy is to be driven back wherever he is found. The columns will march as follows:
>
> 1. Bothmer's Bavarian Division will continue as advanced guard, move on Weissenburg and endeavour to gain possession of the town … It will move at 6 a.m.
>
> 2. The remainder of Hartmann's Corps will leave its bivouac at 4 a.m. and move *via* Bergzabern on Ober Otterbach …
>
> 3. The 4th Cavalry Division will concentrate to the South of Morlheim at 6 a.m. and march *via* Billigheim as far as Ober Otterbach …
>
> 4. The Vth Corps will leave Billigheim at 4 a.m. and march *via* Barbelroth and Nieder Otterbach to Gross Steinfeld and Kapsweyer. It will form its own advanced guard, which will cross the Lauter at St. Remy and Wooghausern, and place outposts on the heights on the far side …
>
> 5. The XIth Corps will start at 4 a.m. and move *via* Steinweiler, Winden, Schaidt across the Bienwald to the Bienwald Hut. It will form its own advanced guard, which will press forward over the Lauter and place outposts on the heights on the further bank …
>
> 6. Werder's Corps will march along the main road to Lauterburg and endeavour to gain possession of that town and place outposts on the far bank …
>
> 7. Von d. Tann's Corps will move at 4 a.m. along the main road *via* Rulzheim to Langenkandel …
>
> 8. My position in the forenoon will be on the heights between Kapsweyer and Schweigen …
>
> (Signed) Frederick William, Crown Prince.

It will be noted that these orders follow closely the main idea underlying Moltke's strategy, namely, to seek out the enemy and destroy him.

The timing of the marches of the different corps is laid down with some precision for the double reason of preventing congestion in the neighbourhood of Landau and of ensuring the simultaneous arrival of the leading troops on the Lauter. If the times and distances are worked out on the assumption that the leading troops started from the places indicated in the orders, it will be found that Bothmer's Bavarian Division might expect to reach Weissenburg at 7.45 a.m., the advanced guard of the Vth Corps to reach Kapsweyer at 7 a.m. and the advanced guard of the XIth Corps to reach the Lauter at 7 a.m. But the order stated that the Vth and XIth Corps were to form their own advanced guards. This order was differently interpreted in the two Corps. The 42nd Brigade, which had been covering the concentration, formed the XIth Corps advanced guard and started from Winden 5 miles ahead of the main body, while the advanced guard of the Vth Corps started from the bivouac of the corps at the hour named in the order. The timing was therefore upset. Adherence to the provisions of our Field Service Regulations for naming a starting-point and the time for the head of the main body to pass that point would prevent such a contretemps.

As the 4th Bavarian Division marched level with the heads of the Vth and XIth Corps it is difficult to see how it could perform the functions of an advanced guard to the army as stated in the order.

The cavalry marched late owing to their position in the midst of the army, and no effort seems to have been made to get them ahead and free of the congestion of traffic that encompassed them.

French plan of Campaign

We have considered in outline the concentration of the German Army and the measures taken to cover the concentration during the critical period before the army was assembled and ready to advance. It is outside the scope of this work to attempt a detailed criticism of the arrangements, but although it is not suggested that they were by any means perfect, it must be borne in mind that as compared with other armies, the state of preparedness of the German Army was greatly in advance of the times.

The organization and the arrangements for mobilization of the French Army were in no sense comparable. In the majority of cases the brigades, divisions and corps were formed on mobilization, and the reserves joined their units after they had reached the frontier stations at which the mobilization took place. The arrangements for supply, the assembly of the transport and the issue of stores and equipment all had to be extemporized to a very great extent. To these shortcomings much of the confusion and hesitation of the early days is attributable. Miscalculations are fatal to strategy, and nobody could foresee with any accuracy when any unit or formation would be complete and ready to move.

In such circumstances it is hardly to be wondered at that it is difficult to ascertain what was in reality the Emperor's plan of campaign. The fact is, that during the period before the first battles took place it varied from day to day according to the information received as to the action of his hoped-for allies, the progress made in the mobilization of his own forces and the news of the enemy.

Seven corps were assembled along the frontier from Huningue to Sierk. At one time there was undoubtedly an idea of assuming the offensive and invading South Germany with the object of joining hands with the Austrians. But the Austrian alliance failed the Emperor at the critical moment and the troops were not ready in time to put such a plan in execution. Offensive plans were therefore abandoned and were succeeded by a desire to guard every avenue of approach, so that French territory might not be invaded before the array was ready to act. Such action is, of course, strategic anathema, leading as it must to dispersion of force and facilitating the delivery of a series of crushing blows by the concentrated forces of the enemy.

On the 25th July the Emperor confided to Marshal MacMahon the command of the Ist and VIIth Corps, which formed the right wing of the French Army in Alsace.

The VIIth Corps consisted of 3 divisions, which were assembling at Colmar, Belfort and Lyons respectively.

The Ist Corps, of which MacMahon retained command, consisted of 4 divisions, which all assembled at Strasburg.

The Vth Corps was assembling at Bitche, in order to assure communication between MacMahon in Alsace and the Emperor on the Saar.

MacMahon's army was, therefore, widely scattered. It was also separated from the main army in Lorraine by the Vosges, a formidable military obstacle, and was opposed, as we have seen; by greatly superior hostile forces that were concentrated and likely to assume the offensive at an early date.

Let us consider for a moment the bearing of the Vosges Mountains on this situation. There were three possible uses to which a Commander, situated as was MacMahon, might put this mountain range.

(i) He might take up a position on the eastern spurs of the range on the right flank of the Crown Prince's army if the latter advanced up the left bank of the Rhine on Strasburg.

(ii) He might retire into the mountains, and attempt to make up for his inferiority in numbers by fighting in a difficult terrain.

(iii) He could retire through the mountains while holding the passes, and prepare to attack the enemy as he debouched.

To take these alternatives seriatim:

(i) A position on the eastern spurs of the Vosges such as the Woerth position, would be what is commonly called a flank position with reference to the IIIrd German Army if it advanced south into Alsace. The Crown Prince could not pass MacMahon by in such a position, but must turn aside to attack him. To do otherwise would expose his own communications. But is there any intrinsic merit in such a position strategically?

Clausewitz tells us that the value of a flank position depends entirely on its tactical strength. If it is so strong as to be practically unassailable and the enemy is checked by it, then a great effect has been obtained by a relatively small expenditure of force. "It is the pressure of the finger on the long lever of a sharp bit." But if the enemy is not checked the effect is apt to be delusive. The defender must either issue from his position and attack the enemy or retreat hurriedly by a detour.

If, on the other hand, the position is not tactically strong, it derives no increase of strength from its position on the flank. The enemy will attack and the decision will be arrived at according to the tactical conditions. The relative direction of the lines of communication of the combatants affects only the fruits of the victory.

We must conclude from the above arguments that such a position as that of Woerth should be judged purely on its tactical merits.

(ii) The same authority tells us that a mountain range is suitable for a relative defence but unsuitable for an absolute defence. Or in other words, a mountain range should be used to delay an enemy rather than to fight a "defensive battle in the mountains." It is easy to see the reason when it is pointed out. A small post may acquire extraordinary strength by selecting a good position in a mountainous country. It has, in fact, "a kind of tactical effrontery" and may "exact the military honour of a regular attack."

But the same does not apply to a chain of posts. For while it may be necessary for the attacker to turn the flank of even a small post, it is usually possible to do so, and the strength of the post conferred by its position in the mountains arises from the fact that the turning movement will be more difficult and will take longer than would ordinarily be the case.

But when we consider the strength of a chain of posts it is obvious that the attack can as a rule concentrate adequate forces against any single post that it may select, and in time capture it. The chain once pierced, the effect of the mountains is to make all the other posts uneasy about the security of their retreat, which is thereby hastened. While mountains, therefore, are strong for a purely passive defence, it is clear that the defence can only be temporary. For if we try to fight a defensive battle in the mountains we are met by all the difficulties of movement to a much greater degree than the attack. The attacker, by selecting his point of attack and concentrating his forces against it, has already overcome half the difficulties, while the defender finds that the mountains have a paralysing effect on his efforts to develop a counter offensive. Successful timing is the essence of the counter-attack, but the difficulties of timing are greatly increased by mountainous ground and the absence of good lateral communications.

The crests of the Vosges were, therefore, an unsuitable terrain in which to seek a decision by fighting a defensive battle.

(iii) The last of our alternatives remains, and that is the plan which seemed to offer the best chance of success. A retirement through the Vosges would have brought MacMahon into closer touch with the Emperor, and would have imposed upon the Crown Prince the delicate operation of forcing the passage of the mountains with the prospect of being attacked when he debouched. The mountains could have been utilized, as Clausewitz says, for a relative defence, i.e., for delay, while a favourable opportunity for attack was sought on the far side.

We have already seen how Moltke proposed to deal with this contingency. Should the French cross the Vosges the Crown Prince was to move "along the Palatinate frontier towards the Saar," so as to be in a position to co-operate with the IInd Army by the 9th August.

MacMahon, however, was probably more concerned with getting his troops ready to take the field, and with fears of being forestalled by the enemy, than by such considerations as the above. On the 2nd August he issued orders for a partial concentration. The 3rd Division Ist Corps was to move from Strasburg to Reichshoffen, Niederbronn and Woerth on the 3rd August.

On the 4th August the following moves were to take place:

VIIth Corps. Dumesnil's Division to move by rail from Colmar to Strasburg. Remainder of corps to watch the Trouee de Belfort.

1st Corps. 2nd Division (A. Douay) from Hagenau to Weissenburg and to hold the Pigeonnier Pass.

1st Division (Ducrot) from Reichshoffen to Lembach.
4th Division from Strasburg to Hagenau when relieved by Dumesnil.
Michel's Cavalry Brigade to Brumath.

In consequence of a report received on the evening of the 2nd August that the Germans intended to occupy Weissenburg on the following day the moves arranged for the 4th August were ordered to take place on the 3rd.

The dispositions of the French troops in Alsace on the evening of the 3rd August are shown in Map III, and it is interesting to compare their dispersion with the concentration of the IIIrd German Army at the same time. The reasons for the French dispositions are instructive.

The greater part of the VIIth Corps was detained near Belfort on account of the operations of Colonel von Seubert's detachment on the Upper Rhine. A flying column had been formed under that officer to allay the fears of the South Germans. It was admirably handled and fulfilled its purpose to the letter.

The 1st and 2nd Divisions were ordered to the frontier, primarily to join hands with the troops of the Vth Corps and to prevent an irruption into French territory, and the move was hastened because of a report that the Germans intended to occupy Weissenburg, where much of the bread for the troops was being baked.

So instead of a well thought out scheme for concentrating the available forces, protected by adequate covering troops, with a force of independent cavalry ready to seek information, we have the different corps assembling in widely-scattered areas, portions of the troops detained far from the scene of the coming conflict by the action of an insignificant detachment, and other troops moving auto a dangerously exposed position to prevent the occupation of a frontier town, on which the troops very wrongly depended for their supplies.

The art of assembling an army, protecting it by covering troops and using the cavalry for exploration was indeed not understood in France at that time.

Let us assume that MacMahon was in a position to concentrate the Ist and VIIth Corps and Duhesme's Cavalry Division of 3 brigades by the 1st August. How should he have set about such a task according to the views which prevail on the subject at present?

The two corps consisted of 7 divisions. It may well have been considered essential to leave a detachment to watch the Upper Rhine, the strength of which should have been kept as low as possible. It should not have exceeded a division, and might have been posted at Mulhausen.

Of the remainder, 5 divisions might have been assembled in the area Strasburg-Brumath-Saverne-Mutzig, with 3 divisions in the first line and 2 in second the line.

Ducrot's division might have been placed at Hagenau as advanced guard to the army, furnishing posts on the line Seitz (to watch the bridge over the Rhine), Soultz-Lembach towards Sturtzelbronn, where hands could have been joined with the covering detachments of the Vth Corps.

A portion of the available cavalry might have been associated with these covering troops to assist in the work of protection, say 2 regiments, while the remaining cavalry might have assembled at Reichshoffen with a view to engaging in extended reconnaissance across the frontier when the moment was considered favourable.

OPPOSING ARMIES ON EVENING OF 3rd AUGUST.

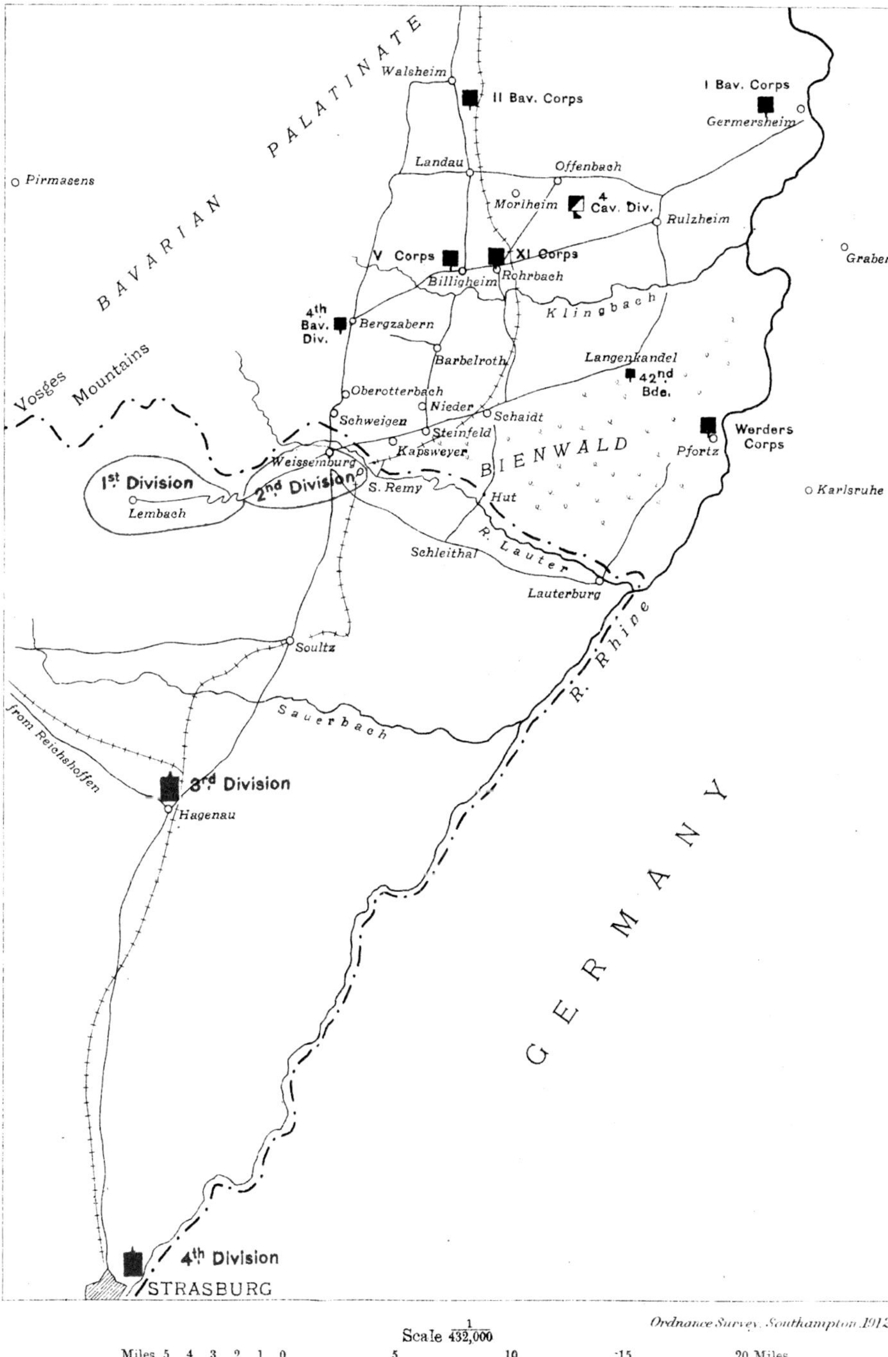

Map III

These suggested dispositions provide a cavalry force suitably placed to engage in reconnaissance when the right moment arrives, a protective screen of posts composed of all arms supported by a division as advanced guard to the army, and the main army disposed in depth so that it can advance, retire, or manœuvre as circumstances may dictate.

The relations between the tasks to be carried out by the independent cavalry and the general advanced guard, and the command of these two forces, are questions of great importance, which are capable of illustration by this example. Is it legitimate to place the independent cavalry and the most advanced infantry formation under one commander and form the whole into a general advanced guard? The answer must depend on the nature of the task that it is intended to assign to the independent cavalry. The tasks of an advanced guard are to protect and to reconnoitre, if necessary, by fighting. It follows that if it is intended to give the independent cavalry a task which might necessitate their moving wide to a flank, leaving the front of the army uncovered, they should not form part of the general advanced guard, or be made subject to the orders of the commander of that force. Conversely, to support the independent cavalry in such circumstances by a force of the other arms might place the supporting force in the position of an isolated detachment.

The independent cavalry should therefore only form part of the general advanced guard and be placed under the orders of the advanced guard commander when the scope of the reconnaissance is restricted, and it is possible to combine the duties of reconnaissance and protection; which is equivalent to saying that the main force of cavalry is no longer independent.

In the case under discussion the area of operations was restricted by the Vosges on the west and the Rhine on the east. A general advanced guard composed of a strong force of cavalry supported by a division, if ordered to move forward towards the Lauter, might well combine the duties of reconnaissance and protection in this restricted area, and act under the orders of a single commander, provided the moment for launching the cavalry was suitably chosen and it was well understood that the distance to which its reconnaissances could be pressed must depend on the capacity of the advanced division to support them while affording the necessary protection to the army. If, on the other hand, it were considered desirable in such a case to employ a strong force of cavalry in reconnaissance beyond the Rhine, it would be very injudicious to support such a reconnaissance by an infantry formation. A dangerously isolated detachment would be formed, and in such a case the action of the infantry should be limited to holding passages over the Rhine, to facilitate the withdrawal of, the cavalry when their task was accomplished.

A good example of the combination of the main cavalry force with a strong force of infantry for the purpose of forming an advanced guard is to be found in the Jena campaign. During the advance of the Grand Army in the celebrated "battalion square" between the 8th and 14th October, Murat's cavalry and Bernadotte's Corps, moving ahead of the centre column, formed the advanced guard of the army. Bernadotte, who was placed by Napoleon under Murat's orders, was half-a-day's march in front of Davout, while the cavalry moved only a short distance ahead of Bernadotte. These dispositions were maintained during the march through the Thuringian Forest and after passing the Saale till the 12th October. Up to that time Napoleon had not divined the Prussian Commander's intention, nor had he located his main forces. Such information as he possessed pointed to the main concentration of the enemy being on the left bank of the Saale. Accordingly he wheeled his army to the left, Davout moving to Naumberg, Lannes to Jena, and Augereau, on the left bank of the Saale, to Calila. But Murat and Bernadotte continued to move north to Zeitz, the light cavalry reconnoitring to the gates of Leipzic. It was not till the 13th October that this advanced guard was broken up and Bernadotte was ordered to join Davout at Naumburg while Murat moved west to the Saale. It was Lannes, therefore, and not Murat, who located Prince Hohenlohe's army at Jena on the 13th October, the cavalry reconnaissances to the north having yielded purely negative information.

The circumstances, however, do not form by any means an exact parallel with those under discussion. While it was necessary for Napoleon's army to traverse the Thuringian Forest, it was uncertain in which direction the enemy would be encountered when the army emerged from the defiles, whether on the right or the left bank of the Saale. If there had been a reasonable certainty that the enemy would concentrate in the district between the Saale and the Elster this close association of Murat and Bernadotte as a general advanced guard to the army would have fulfilled all the requirements of the case. The cavalry could hardly have missed finding the enemy in such a restricted area, and the support of a Corps behind them would have greatly facilitated the pushing back of the enemy's advanced troops and the clearing up of the situation. If the enemy were to assume the offensive the resistance offered by the Corps would have allowed the army to close up and deploy.

Seeing, however, that so much uncertainty existed as to the direction in which the enemy would be found, some explanation must be sought for the limitations placed by Napoleon on the scope of the movements of his cavalry. Two reasons have been assigned for his dispositions. He is said to have wished to profess pacific intentions up to the last possible moment, a consideration which may have influenced him in keeping his cavalry back till the army actually advanced, but could hardly account for the method of their employment after passing the defiles of the forest. The more likely explanation is that he considered the Prussian cavalry superior to his own, and did not wish to run any risk of an initial reverse.

Whatever Napoleon's reasons may have been, it must be admitted that in the circumstances of the case instructions to the cavalry to seek out and locate the enemy's main forces would have accorded better with the views on the subject now held. As such instructions would certainly have taken the bulk of the cavalry to the left bank of the Saale there would have been considerable risk in supporting them with an infantry formation, as was proved by the dangers incurred by Augereau and Lannes when separated from the remainder of the army by the Saale on the 12th and 13th October.

The Advance of the 2nd Division to Weissenburg

We have seen above the circumstances in which the 1st and 2nd Divisions of the 1st Corps moved forward to the frontier on the 3rd August. MacMahon's order of the 2nd August placed both divisions wider the orders of Ducrot, but at the same time the marshal issued orders direct to the 2nd Division as to the position to be occupied at Weissenburg. This led to the receipt of conflicting orders by General Abel Douay.

MacMahon ordered him to put the bulk of his division in Weissenburg and the valley of the Lauter, where they would have been commanded from the high ground to the north of the river which was already occupied by the enemy.

Ducrot ordered him to put a battalion in Weissenburg, to dispose the remainder of his force on the Geisberg ridge to the south of the town and to reconnoitre with his cavalry in the morning.

But what was worse than these conflicting orders was that General Douay was not informed of the object of the move of his division to Weissenburg. His orders did not include instructions as to how he was to act in given circumstances, nor was such information as was available as to the enemy communicated to him. He did not know, therefore, whether there was any likelihood of the enemy assuming the offensive immediately, nor did he know whether, if attacked, he would be supported, or whether he should fight a delaying action and retire. And yet his dispositions should certainly have depended on his intended action if attacked.

The division marched from Hagenau at 4 a.m. but waited for five hours at Soultz for supplies and stores expected to arrive by train, which never arrived. In the end the troops reached their destination at 8.30 p.m., the cavalry having marched all the way behind the infantry.

General Douay made the following dispositions:

Headquarters at Steinseltz

1st Brigade (General Montmarie)

50th Regiment.	2 battns. Geisberg Plateau.
	1 battn. Seltz.
74th Regiment.	2 battns. Geisberg Plateau.
	1 battn. Weissenburg.

2nd Brigade (General Pellé).

78th Regiment	} near Shafbusch Farm
1st Turcos	}
Divisional Artillery	{2 field batteries} between the 1st and 2nd Brigades.
	{1 machine gun b'y)}

Septeuil's Cavalry Brigade.

11th Chasseurs near the Geisberg.

3rd Hussars, 4 squadrons at Rott, 1 squadron on Pigeonnier Pass.

The outposts were placed close round camp, owing to the late arrival.

The nearest troops were:

1st Division on the line Pigeonnier, Climbach, Lembach.

3rd Division at Reichshoffen.

4th Division at Strasburg.

The only troops, therefore, that could possibly come to the assistance of the Division if attacked were portions of the 1st Division.

The ground

The town of Weissenburg is situated on the Lauter, a tributary of the Rhine, having its source in the Vosges Mountains. The stream is fordable in places with difficulty. The town is an old dismantled fortress and in 1870 was still surrounded by lines, consisting of an infantry parapet and ditch, which made a formidable obstacle.

The Lauter runs between two spurs of the Vosges known as the Geisberg and Wolfsberg ridges. The hills from which these spurs protrude are densely wooded and crossed only by mountain paths, the spurs themselves being cultivated and covered with crops, vineyards and hop-gardens.

The open space between the wooded Vosges Mountains and the extensive forest of the Bienwald is not more than 2½ miles in width. In this open space the tactical features of importance are:

North of the Lauter – the village of Schweigen, the Wolfsberg and its under feature the Windhof.

South of the Lauter – the Weiler ravine, steep, almost precipitous – the Weissenburg railway station and the walled enclosure to the east of it – Altenstadt – St. Remy – the bifurcation of the railway lines – the Vogelsberg – the Geisberg Plateau – the Geisberg – the Gutleithof and the Schafbusch Farm.

The roads by which the Germans advanced were:

(i) Ober Otterbach – Schweigen.
(ii) Steinfeld-Sweighofen.
(iii) Schaidt-Schleithal.

Those available for the French to retire by were:

(i) Via the Pigeonnier.
(ii) Via Rott and the Pfaffenschlick Pass.
(iii) Via Riedseltz and the Strasburg Road.

The battle

At 4 a.m. General Douay sent out a reconnaissance consisting of 1 battalion, 2 squadrons and a section of artillery. The battalion and the guns took up a position half-way down the Geisberg ridge above Altenstadt. The cavalry went down the road leading to the Hagenau gate of Weissenburg, then took the Lauterburg road, turned off to the north by the road to Landau and moved towards the frontier to the south of Schweigen. Having heard from the inhabitants that 30,000 Prussians had left Landau and were approaching Weissenburg, they turned eastwards along the frontier and returned by the Kapsweyer road, reaching camp at 7.30 a.m. They had seen only a few German patrols and had taken no steps to verify the information obtained from the inhabitants or to disprove it.

The head of the advanced guard of the 4th Bavarian Division, consisting of 2 squadrons, 2 battalions and a battery, reached Schweigen at 8 a.m. and as soon as the southern exit of the village was reached the French troops in Weissenburg and on the Geisberg ridge became visible. The advanced guard battery, escorted by 1 battalion, came into action 600 yards south of Schweigen and opened fire on the town at 8.30 a.m. with the result that the French troops in Weissenburg at once manned the parapet of the old lines, a battery (Captain Didier) came into action just south of the railway station and General Pellé ordered the 3 battalions of the 1st Turcos into the valley, 2 battalions going to the east of the town and 1 battalion to the west.

General Bothmer, commanding the 4th Bavarian Division, then brought a second battery into action, supported on the left by a battalion of the 5th Regiment, and ordered the 10th Chasseurs to work through the vineyards towards the Bitche gate of the town. The superior fire of the Bavarian artillery caused the Didier battery to retire 500 yards, but the infantry made very slow progress.

About this time Bothmer received a report that a considerable force of French infantry could be seen moving on the heights beyond Weissenburg, apparently with the intention of attacking his right flank. These troops were probably 2 battalions, 78th Regiment, marching up the road to the Pigeonnier Pass to relieve the 96th Regiment, in accordance with orders received from General Ducrot. The anxiety caused by this report led Bothmer to send 1 battalion to the Schloss St. Paul, 14 battalions towards Guttenburg and Dorrenbach (in the mountains to the north-west of Schweigen) and 1 battalion to the west of Schweigen to protect his right. This left him with only 2 battalions in hand, which were drawn up just south of Schweigen.

The fire of a French battery in action near the 3 Poplars, coupled with that of the Dither battery, now in action again, had already caused the withdrawal of the 2 Bavarian batteries south of Schweigen, although their losses had been slight. The offensive of the 4th Bavarian Division was thus held in check up till 10.30 a.m.

The advanced guard of the Vth Corps reached Schweighofen at 8.30 a.m. Here it separated into two portions:

3 squadrons }
3 battalions } under Colonel Rex moved on St. Remy
1 battery }
1 squadron }
3 battalions } under Colonel Bothmer moved on Wooghausern
1 battery }

The head of the main body had now reached Klein-Steinfeld, where the sound of the guns could be heard, so General von Kirchbach, commanding the Vth Corps, sent to General Bothmer to ask how he could best assist him. The latter replied that he was uneasy about his right flank and that the Vth Corps would help him best by bringing pressure to bear on the enemy's right.

The Crown Prince arrived at Schweigen at 9.15 a.m. and sent to the commanders of the Vth and XIth Corps to hurry them up.

The advanced guard of the XIth Corps reached Bienwald Hut at 7 a.m. and crossed the Lauter at once. By 8.30 a.m. the 42nd Brigade had occupied the Schleithal heights. The sound of the firing was now heard, and General Von Bose, commanding the Corps, left the 42nd Brigade in position and diverted the march of the 41st Brigade by the Lauterburg road on Altenstadt. It will be seen that this Brigade was now about to clash with the advanced guard of the Vth Corps. Colonel Bothmer's portion of the Vth Corps advanced guard had not heard the firing, and remained in the valley of the Lauter till 11 a.m. Von Bose, however, met Colonel Rex and arranged with him that the Vth Corps should move on Altenstadt, while the XIth Corps moved south through the Niederwald to attack the enemy's right flank on the Geisberg ridge.

At 10.30 a.m. General Bothmer considered that the Vth Corps had made sufficient progress to justify him in renewing the offensive. He therefore launched 3 battalions, with 2 battalions in second line, supported by 2 batteries on the Windhof against the 2 battalions of the Turcos in the valley east of Weissenburg. At the same time Rex's Column advancing through Altehstadt assailed these same battalions in flank. A most stubborn fight ensued, the Turcos being gradually pressed back by superior numbers on the railway station and a walled enclosure to the east of it.

We must now turn for a moment to the French side.

Although General Douay had received a telegram from MacMahon at 6 a.m. warning him to look out for an attack by superior forces, the French were completely surprised when the advanced guard battery of the 4th Bavarian Division opened fire on Weissenburg. The troops stood to arms, and in the absence of General Douay, who was at Steinseltz, General Pellé ordered the Ist Turcos and the Didier battery into the valley as has already been described. At the same time General Montmarie ordered the 1st and 3rd battalions, 50th Regiment, to take post covering the Geisberg, facing east and north. These two battalions took up their positions about 200 yards down the slope of the ridge, with skirmishers to the front. The reserves, cavalry and artillery, took post behind the slope of the ridge.

Such was the position of affairs at 9 a.m. when General Douay appeared on the field. He approved of the dispositions of his subordinates, and telegraphed to MacMahon informing him of the situation that had arisen. The first steps taken by Douay were to send a cavalry officers' patrol, supported by a squadron to reconnoitre towards the Niederwald, and to order the remaining batteries of the divisional artillery into action. The officers' patrol, after being fired on, returned, reporting that they had seen a division of the enemy. The two batteries, one of which was a machine gun battery, came into action 500 yards north of the 3 Poplars.

We have already seen how the French artillery were successful in causing the withdrawal of the 2 batteries of the 4th Bavarian Division. Their success was short lived, for the Germans brought 5 batteries into action on the Windhof, the 2 batteries belonging to the advanced guards of the Vth Corps in the angle formed by the railway lines, and two batteries of the XIth Corps east of the Gutleithof. This greatly superior force of artillery had all the advantages of a converging fire, and very soon reduced the French artillery to impotence.

At 10.30 a.m. it was clear to Douay that his right flank was threatened by a greatly superior force and that his retreat would be compromised if much longer delayed. He therefore gave the order for the 2nd Brigade and the battalion of the 74th Regiment forming the garrison of Weissenburg to retire. Immediately afterwards he was killed by a shrapnel bullet, while near the artillery position at the 3 Poplars.

The command devolved upon General Pellé, who was at the time occupied with the fight in the valley. He received the order from General Douay to retire, but owing to their being engaged at very close quarters, he judged it impossible to extricate the 2nd and 3rd battalions of the 1st Turcos without the assistance of fresh troops. He therefore sent to the 4th Battalion, now west of the town, to move to the east, and cover the withdrawal of the other two battalions. This took some time to carry out, and in the meanwhile the 2nd and 3rd battalions were assailed by greatly superior forces, in front by the Bavarians and in flank by the troops of Rex's advanced guard. In spite of the most heroic resistance and more than one successful counterstroke they were eventually driven into a confined space about the railway station.

Shortly after 12 o'clock the 4th Battalion was in position and the 2nd and 3rd battalions withdrew to their camp on the Geisberg ridge, where they struck their tents, replenished their ammunition, put on their kits and marched off in good order to the Pfaffenschlick Pass. Their losses had been very heavy, but their moral was quite unshaken.

BATTLE OF WEISSEMBURG. SITUATION 10 A. M.

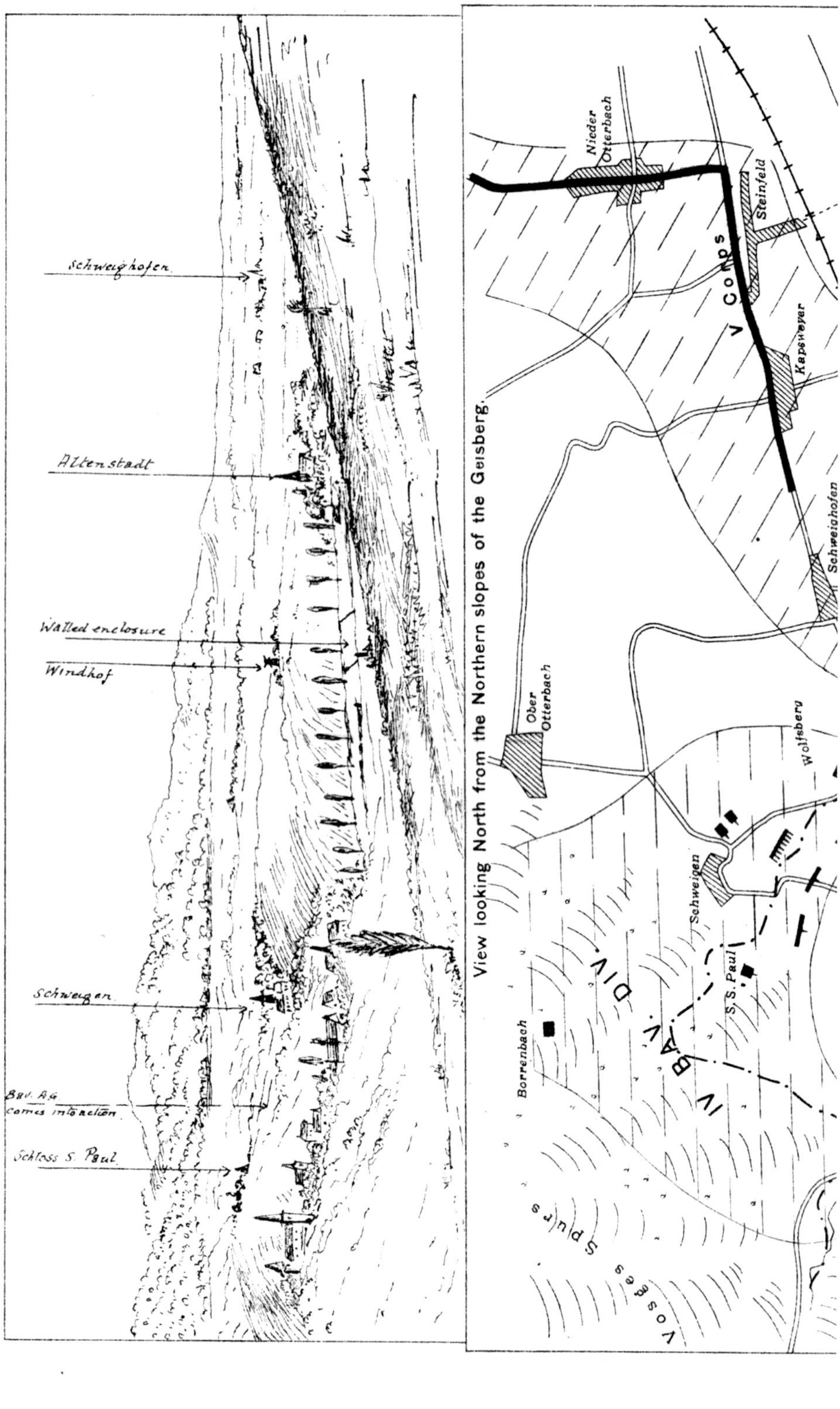

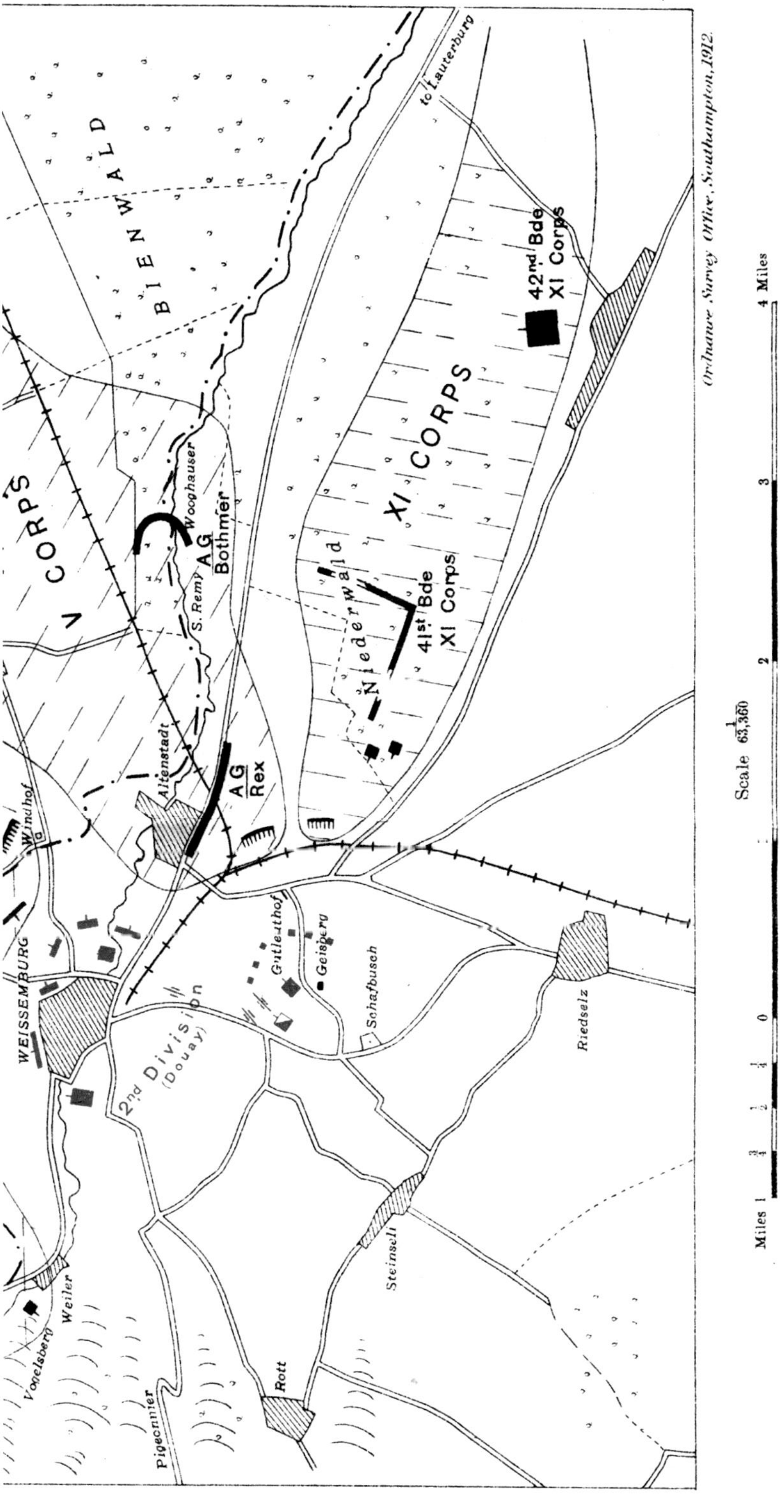
BIENWALD
V CORPS
XI CORPS
42nd Bde XI Corps
41st Bde XI Corps
Niederwald
AG Bothmer
AG Rex
Woghauser
S. Remy
Altenstadt
Windhof
WEISSEMBURG
Gutleuthof
Geisberg
Schafbusch
2nd Division (Douay)
Riedselz
Steinselt
Rott
Weiler
Vogelsberg
Pigeonnier
to Lauterburg
Ordnance Survey Office, Southampton, 1912.
Scale $\frac{1}{63,360}$
Miles 1 0 1 2 3 4 Miles

Map IV

The Didier battery, which had done its best to support the Turcos to the last moment, withdrew at the same time up to the crest of the ridge.

It was not till after 12 o'clock that Pellé heard of the death of Douay. He at once went to the Geisberg Plateau to supervise the arrangements for retreat. But it now became apparent that the force was so deeply implicated that it could not be hastily withdrawn. There had been delay in getting the transport clear and it was blocking the roads. The fight in the valley, moreover, had been so prolonged that the attack on the right flank was already beginning to take effect.

Pellé consulted Septeuil as to what use could be made of the cavalry, and they both agreed that the ground was unsuitable for cavalry action. The Brigade was therefore ordered to retire *via* Steinseltz. The artillery were also ordered to withdraw to the Steinseltz ridge to cover the retirement of the infantry. They got away with the loss of one gun, which was disabled.

Interest now centred round the Geisberg. The situation in the neighbourhood of the chateau was as follows:

The 1st Battalion, 50th Regiment, posted east of the Geisberg, and the 3rd Battalion, 50th Regiment, and the 3rd Battalion, 74th Regiment, to the north of the chateau, were attacked on the east by the 41st Brigade, XIth Corps, and on the north by Rex and Bothmer, Vth Corps. They were subject also to a converging artillery fire.

The 1st Battalion, 74th Regiment, up to now in reserve, was deployed to help the retirement of the 1st Battalion, 50th Regiment. General Montmarie was successful in extricating the 3rd Battalion, 50th Regiment, and the 3rd Battalion, 74th Regiment, and they retired to the Shafbusch farm. The other two battalions, however, became very hotly engaged, and when they retired about 200 men took refuge in the Geisberg instead of withdrawing with their battalions.

Commandant Cecile was in command at the Geisberg. He now organized the defenders, who gave a good account of themselves. The chateau is a naturally strong place, practically proof against assault, but as it was clear that it must eventually be surrounded, Commandant Cecile decided to attempt to break out towards the 3 Poplars. He rode out gallantly at the head of his men and was killed 50 yards from the gate. The men then withdrew again into the chateau. In spite of repeated attempts and heavy losses it was found impossible to capture the place till artillery had been brought up and the gate blown in. At 3 p.m. the garrison surrendered, 200 unwounded prisoners being taken.

Meanwhile the debris of the 4 battalions of the 50th and 74th Regiments had reformed at the Shafbusch Farm, where they were attacked by the troops pressing on after the capture of the Geisberg and by troops of the 41st Brigade now moving up the Riedseltz valley. The Germans assaulted and captured the farm, the French retiring in disorder, some by Kleebourg and the Pfaffenschlick Pass and others by Soultz to Hagenau.

The 4th Cavalry Division had been delayed at Billigheim and touch was lost before the Crown Prince ordered a regiment of divisional cavalry to pursue. This regiment went as far as Soultz, which was found to be occupied, so they returned to make their report.

Douay's order to the Commandant of Weissenburg to withdraw the garrison was delivered by the Staff Officer sent with the message to a NCO at the gate of the town and did not reach the Commandant till 1 p.m. By that time retirement was impossible, and after trying vainly to break out at the different gates of the town the garrison surrendered.

Chapter II

Comments on the Battle of Weissenburg

The causes of the defeat of the 2nd Division

The consideration of the causes of the defeat of the 2nd Division will be facilitated if answers can be found to the following questions:

(i) Why was the division placed in such an exposed position, beyond the reach of support?

(ii) How did it come to allow itself to be surprised?

(iii) Why was it unable to break off the action and retire without suffering complete defeat?

(i) We have already seen how haphazard were the arrangements for the concentration of the French Army, and how unsuitable were the dispositions for covering that concentration. There was a complete absence of carefully thought out plans, put into execution with business-like determination. The movements of such troops as were ready to take the field were governed by the latest rumour, and questions connected with the supply and equipment of the troops were sometimes a compelling cause. But at the root of the whole evil was the false strategical conception of trying to guard all avenues of approach, and prevent the invasion of French territory. It is not suggested that the frontier should not have been closely watched, but the forces employed on or close to the frontier were out of all proportion to the necessities of the cases. The bulk of the army was employed in screening, and there was little left to screen.

We must condemn, therefore, as unsound, the move of the 1st and 2nd Divisions to the frontier on the 3rd August, and we must also condemn the indefinite nature of the instructions issued by Marshal MacMahon and General Ducrot to General Douay. Had the last-named officer known definitely that he was placed at Weissenburg as an advanced guard to cover the concentration of the army he would have known exactly how to dispose his troops and how to act in the varying circumstances that might arise. There is, however, no indication that Douay ever received such instructions, and the answer to our question must be that the division was thrust forward into a dangerously isolated position in pursuance of the false strategical principle of attempting to guard every avenue of approach.

(ii) The division was surprised in its bivouac owing to the inadequacy of the cavalry reconnaissances. Septeuil's Cavalry Brigade had been placed by Ducrot under Douay's immediate orders. It was available on the 3rd August to move ahead of the 2nd Division to the frontier and carry out reconnaissances across the Lauter. If the brigade had been handled on the 3rd in accordance with the principles laid down in our Field Service Regulations for the employment of independent cavalry for exploration, officers' patrols, supported by contact squadrons, could have penetrated between the German covering detachments, and the bulk of the brigade could have been kept concentrated, either to support the reconnoitring detachments, to form a rallying point on which they could fall back, or to engage any hostile force of cavalry that endeavoured to prevent the carrying out of their mission. There was no force of hostile cavalry nearer than the 4th Cavalry Division at Billigheim, and that division appears to have been ill prepared at the moment to undertake active operations. Instead of acting as suggested Septeuil's Cavalry Brigade marched to Weissenburg in rear of the 2nd Division, and reached the Geisberg plateau after dark.

But even on the morning of the 4th August it was not too late to avert a surprise, and moreover Ducrot's orders to Douay were to use the cavalry to reconnoitre beyond Weissenburg or in the direction of Lauterburg. The reconnaissance actually conducted by 2 squadrons on the morning of the 4th August was puerile in its conception as well as in its execution, and its insufficiency was the immediate cause of the division being surprised. For this General Douay must be held responsible.

(iii) When the first shot was fired by the advanced guard battery of the 4th Bavarian Division General Douay was at his Headquarters at Steinseltz. General Pellé acted on a soldierly impulse and ordered the 3 battalions of the 1st Turcos into the valley to engage the enemy. In such circumstances it is not possible to quarrel with his decision to obtain further information as to the situation by getting into touch with the enemy at once. But it is very questionable whether it was advisable to implicate such a large proportion of the available infantry in the valley at the outset. However, owing to the somewhat feeble conduct of the preliminary operations by the 4th Bavarian Division, no great harm resulted from Pellé's action up to 10.30 a.m. At that hour Douay, who had obtained information by means of a cavalry officers' patrol, which confirmed his fears for the safety of his right flank, gave the order to retire. This order was timely, but the gallant General's death was most untimely, and was the direct cause of the severe reverse suffered by the division.

Pellé was engaged with the Turcos in the valley, and such a large force was now implicated in a fight at close quarters, that he judged it impossible to withdraw without support. He therefore sent for the 4th Battalion to come to the support of the 2nd and 3rd Battalions. This took an hour to carry out, and in the meanwhile every minute's delay made the withdrawal of the 2nd and 3rd Battalions more difficult, added to the casualties, and enabled the Germans to get to closer grips with the right wing on the Geisberg ridge. If only 1 battalion had been engaged in the valley in the first instance, supported by a second battalion, Douay's orders for the retirement could have been carried out without delay, the right could easily have maintained itself till the troops in the valley were clear, and the division could have withdrawn having fulfilled the functions of an advanced guard. That is to say, it would have compelled the greater part of the greatly superior German Army to deploy, would have reconnoitred its strength and divined its purpose, and would have withdrawn with slight loss, having inflicted greater loss on its opponents and delayed their march.

But in the French Army of those days only two kinds of action were understood, to attack or to defend. To delay the enemy by manœuvre, to make him take 3 or 4 hours to advance 3 or 4 miles was a forgotten art.

In the words of our Field Service Regulations: "The guiding principle in all delaying action must be that when the enemy has liberty to manœuvre, the passive occupation of a position, however strong, can rarely be justified, and always involves the risk of crushing defeat under these conditions a delaying force must manoeuvre, so as to force the enemy to deploy as often as possible, but should rarely accept battle."

The occupation of the ground by the French

As an academic exercise it is interesting to consider how the ground could be occupied to the best advantage, with a view to fighting a delaying action against superior forces.

We must remember that the crest of the Schweigen ridge was occupied by the enemy's covering troops, and that there were urgent reasons connected with supply for occupying Weissenburg.

These conditions indicate the desirability of keeping the bulk of the troops as much concealed as possible under cover of the Geisberg ridge, while a suitable portion of the force, say 1½ to 2 battalions, takes up the best outpost position available. The choice of this outpost position is a matter open to discussion, but a suitable arrangement would appear to be to occupy Weissenburg, Altenstadt and the Gutleithof as advanced posts. Weissenburg would not require to be artificially strengthened, but the outskirts of Altenstadt and the Gutleithof should be placed in a state of defence with the assistance of the engineers, and troops should be economized by connecting these posts only lightly, for to penetrate between them before they had been captured would not be an easy operation.

Localities such as the Geisberg and the Shafbusch Farm should be placed in a state of defence, and some trenches might well be prepared on the Vogelsberg and on the high ground south-west of Weissenburg covering the roads leading up the Pigeonnier and to Rott. Alternative emplacements should be prepared for the artillery facing north and east.

These dispositions would prevent surprise and keep the strength of the force concealed from the enemy. They would compel the enemy to deploy on a broad front at a considerable distance from the main body and allow his strength to be reconnoitred by the advanced posts before they gave way. The withdrawal of the advanced posts could be covered by artillery fire, and finally the main force could retire in successive echelons from the right, provided it was intended to retreat by either the Pfaffenschlick or Pigeonnier passes, or from the left if it was intended to retire by Soultz.

When it became necessary to occupy the position firing lines should be formed, and for that matter trenches should have been sited, with a good field of fire at distant and medium ranges, dead ground immediately to the front being of little importance. Such positions have the effect of protecting the infantry from the fire of the attacking artillery, which will probably be very superior to that of the defence, and facilitate withdrawal. Positions well down the forward slope, such as those taken up by the 50th and 74th Regiments for the defence of the Geisberg ridge, have, on the other hand, every disadvantage when the object is only to delay.

As regards the choice of the line of retreat, the right flank is much more easily assailable than the left, which can only be approached over the steep and thickly-wooded spurs of the Vosges and the precipitous Weiler ravine. Everything points, therefore, to retreat by the passes into the Lembach valley and not by the road to Soultz.

Failure of the French troops in the vicinity of the battlefield to support the 2nd Division

The 78th Regiment, belonging to the 2nd Division, left the Geisberg plateau at 5 a.m. on the 4th August, in accordance with orders from General Ducrot, to relieve the 96th

Regiment belonging to the 1st Division, which was posted at Klimbach and was holding the Pigeonnier and Pfaffenschlick passes. The 96th Regiment when relieved was to move further west to Wingen at the head of the Lembach valley. This disposition, it will be noted, while it tended to concentrate the 1st Division, had the opposite effect as regards the 2nd Division and deprived General Douay of a considerable portion of his available infantry.

The 78th Regiment climbed to the summit of the Pigeonnier Pass, and by 8 a.m. the bulk of the regiment had reached Klimbach, having left several observation posts on the passes. The sound of the guns at Weissenburg was clearly audible at Klimbach, and the progress of the battle could be watched distinctly with glasses from the Pigeonnier. But the regiment remained inactive throughout the day, and its commander did not even think of sending a mounted officer to General Douay for orders. Possibly he was satisfied with carrying out the orders which he had already received, but when General Ducrot issued instructions for him to relieve the 96th Regiment, he was certainly not aware that the 2nd Division would be attacked next day. It was the duty of the commander of the 78th Regiment to act on his own judgment, and it is only possible to conclude either that his judgment was at fault or that he failed in his duty.

The 96th Regiment was to move to Wingen. The sound of the guns was heard "during the morning," the move was stopped and the regiment awaited orders, the commander reporting to General Ducrot at 11 a.m. This commanding officer also failed to exercise an initiative which was well within his province, namely, to march to the scene of action.

General Ducrot met Marshal MacMahon on the summit of the Pigeonnier during the early hours of the afternoon, but by that time it was too late to succour the 2nd Division.

The Action of the 4th Bavarian Division

A difficult problem presented itself for solution by the commander of the advanced guard of the 4th Bavarian Division when his troops passed through Schweigen and discovered a considerable force of the enemy in their immediate front, wholly unaware of their presence. The arrival of Douay's Division at Weissenburg had not been reported to General Bothmer by his advanced posts, and the Bavarians were as much surprised as the French when they came upon the enemy.

It was imperative to make the most of this unexpected situation. The first object should have been to avoid giving the enemy premature warning, and the second to make use of the advantages conferred by surprise to prevent his escape. The first of these objects should have instilled caution, and the withholding of fire of all sorts till a sufficient force was at hand and deployed ready to make a vigorous holding attack. At the same rime the enemy might have become aware of his perilous situation at any moment, and the sooner he was attacked the less likely it was that he would escape the inevitable confusion that results from being surprised.

These considerations are conflicting and the time that can be devoted to preparation before fire is opened must in such circumstances be a matter of judgment. In this case it must be admitted that the action of the artillery of the advanced guard in taking up a position within long, range rifle fire of the Weissenburg lines and opening fire on the town before any considerable body of infantry was ready to press the attack was premature and ill-advised. It served only to alarm the enemy.

In extenuation it may be argued that it was the opening of Artillery fire on the town which drew the Turcos into the valley, and that again this contributed greatly to the difficulty experienced by the French in withdrawing. But it has already been shown that up till 10.30 a.m. the French were free to withdraw, and would have done so if General Douay had not been killed. This argument must therefore be dismissed.

The somewhat feeble efforts of the infantry of the division to get to close quarters with the enemy in Weissenburg corresponded no better to the necessities of the situation.

Once having alarmed the enemy it was essential to attack with vigour and hold him to his ground, and the most energetic action possible was called for. It cannot be said that it was forthcoming. Instead of concentrating his energies on a vigorous attack, General Bothmer seems to have been inspired by the fear of what the forest-clad mountains on his right flank might contain, and this fear of the unknown, fostered by the report of a movement of French infantry in a westerly direction, caused him to disseminate a great part of his force for purely protective purposes. There was as a fact, little justification for his fears. Although the French were known to be in strength at Bitche, the approach to Bothmer's right flank must necessarily have been through the most difficult country, passable only for small forces of infantry and quite impracticable for the co-operation of the arms. An attack in force was not to be expected and the situation would have been adequately met by reconnaissances on the part of the divisional cavalry along the few mountain paths that led in a north-westerly direction.

It is also impossible to justify the withdrawal of the 2 batteries of artillery from action south of Schweigen after losing 1 man killed and 8 wounded.

The exercise of command by the Crown Prince, the co-operation of the subordinate German Commanders and the impetuosity of the attack

The only recorded orders of the Crown Prince on the field of battle are those sent when he first arrived at Schweigen at 9.15 a.m. to hurry up the Vth and XIth Corps, and the order to the 4th Regiment of Dragoons to pursue the enemy at the close of the action. Was it not possible or desirable for him to intervene with greater effect?

The spirit of loyal co-operation which inspired the corps commanders brought them to the scene of the action without orders, and they at once consulted one another as to the most suitable action to be taken. For instance, the commander of the Vth Corps asked the commander of the 4th Bavarian Division how he could best assist him, and acted at once on his suggestion; the commander of the XIth Corps consulted Colonel Rex, and diverted the march of his leading troops so that they should not clash with those of the Vth Corps.

Probably no orders issued by the Crown Prince could have reached the corps commanders in time to better the action taken by them spontaneously. But when the enemy's advanced troops had been driven from the valley and it became necessary to press the attack on the Geisberg ridge, an opportunity seems to have been afforded for the effective intervention of the Commander. The German casualties at Weissenburg were very heavy and amounted to nearly 90 officers and 1,500 men. These heavy losses were greatly due to the precipitate manner in which the troops were thrown into the fight and the way in which the action was allowed to develop with little or no preparation. This was particularly the case in the attack on the Geisberg. It was a naturally strong tactical point, proof against assault, and it was essential to prepare the attack with artillery fire. The Geisberg and the Shafbusch farms acted as magnets to the attack, and no use was made of the great superiority of force available to envelop completely the enemy's position.

Surely here was an opportunity for the timely intervention of the Commander, in order to co-ordinate the efforts of the different corps and assure the success of the operation without undue haste and undue losses. Portions of the XIth Corps might have been directed on Riedseltz, and, while this turning movement was developing, the attack of the Vth Corps on the Geisberg and the Shafbusch farms might have been adequately prepared. It may be argued that any delay would have afforded to the enemy the opportunity of escape from their uncomfortable situation. This would only have been the case if the turning movement had been arrested and the frontal attack had ceased to be pressed. As long as the turning movement continued without interruption it promised in the end greater results than a direct attack, and it would surely have been possible to press the frontal attack sufficiently to prevent the enemy's escape without actually assaulting the Geisberg before the attack on it had been adequately prepared.

Impetuosity is a good fault, but it leads to heavy casualties, and on this occasion it led also to the mixing of units and to a degree of confusion that might well have prejudiced the success of the operation if the enemy's force had not been numerically insignificant.

The Crown Prince failed to organize an effective pursuit. The 4th Cavalry Division had been delayed at Billigheim, and the order sent to bring it forward to the neighbourhood of Altenstadt failed to reach it in time. But in the absence of the 4th Cavalry Division a considerable force of Divisional Cavalry might still have been collected, and to employ a single cavalry regiment for this purpose must be looked upon as totally inadequate. For the regiment to abandon touch with the enemy and return "to report" was inexcusable.

Chapter III

5th August

German advance

On the night of the 4th August after the battle the IIIrd German Army was disposed as follows:

IInd Bavarian Corps	}
Vth Corps	} in bivouac on the battlefield, south of
XIth Corps	} the Lauter
Ist Bavarian Corps	Laugenkandel
Werder's Corps	Lauterburg
4th Cavy. Divn.	Ober Otterbach
Headquarters	Schweighofen

Orders were issued by the Crown Prince in the evening for the army to continue its march on Strasburg on the following day.

The 4th Cavalry Division was ordered to advance by Altenstadt and the Hagenau high road, and reconnoitre in the direction of Hagenau, Suffelnheim and Roppenheim, i.e. to the south, with one regiment towards Woerth and Reichsoffen. This reconnaissance was carried out by General Bernhardi with a brigade of Uhlans, and obtained the information that a considerable French force was camped on the heights of Froeschweiler and the Morsbronn ridge beyond the Gunstett bridge, and that Hagenau was occupied by hostile infantry. The division bivouacked at Hunspach.

The destinations of the corps were as follows:–

Ist Bavarian Corps	Ingolsheim
IInd Bavarian Corps	Lembach
Vth Corps	Preuschdorf
XIth Corps	Soultz
Werder's Corps	Aschbach

Headquarters were to move to Soultz.

The Staff arrangements for the march were defective, and the troops consequently suffered much unnecessary fatigue. For instance, the Vth, XIth and Werder's Corps marched by the same road, which caused the very late arrival of the last-named corps at its destination, while some units of the Ist Bavarian Corps did not reach their bivouac till midnight.

It should be noted that the disposition of the army was such as to permit of the resumption of the march on the following day in either a westerly or southerly direction, which conformed with the somewhat uncertain information as to the enemy.

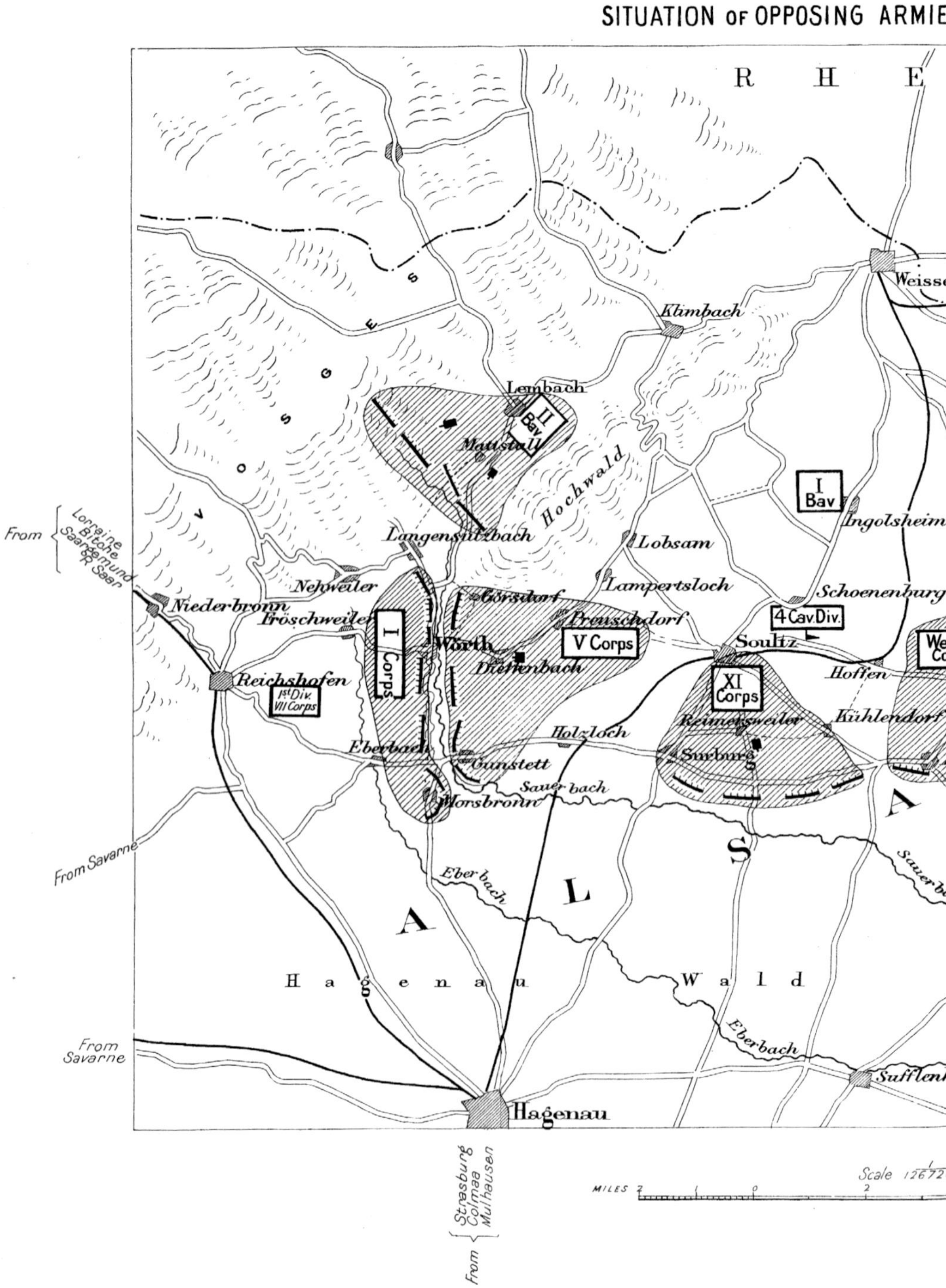
SITUATION OF OPPOSING ARMIES
R H E
VOSGES
Weissen
Klimbach
Lembach
II Bav
Mattstall
Hochwald
I Bav
Ingolsheim
From Lorraine Bitche Saargemund Saar R
Langensulzbach
Lobsam
Lampertsloch
Nehweiler
Niederbronn
Görsdorf
Schoenenburg
Fröschweiler
Preuschdorf
4 Cav.Div.
I Corps
Wörth
V Corps
Soultz
Dieffenbach
Reichshofen
XI Corps
Hoffen
1st Div. VII Corps
Reimersweiler
Kühlendorf
Holzloch
Eberbach
Surburg
Gunstett
Sauer bach
Morsbronn
From Savarne
Eberbach
A L S A
Sauerbach
Hagenau Wald
Eberbach
From Savarne
Sufflenh
Hagenau
From Strasburg Colmaa Mulhausen
MILES 2 1 0 2
Scale

Map V

S ON THE NIGHT OF THE 5/6 AUGUST.

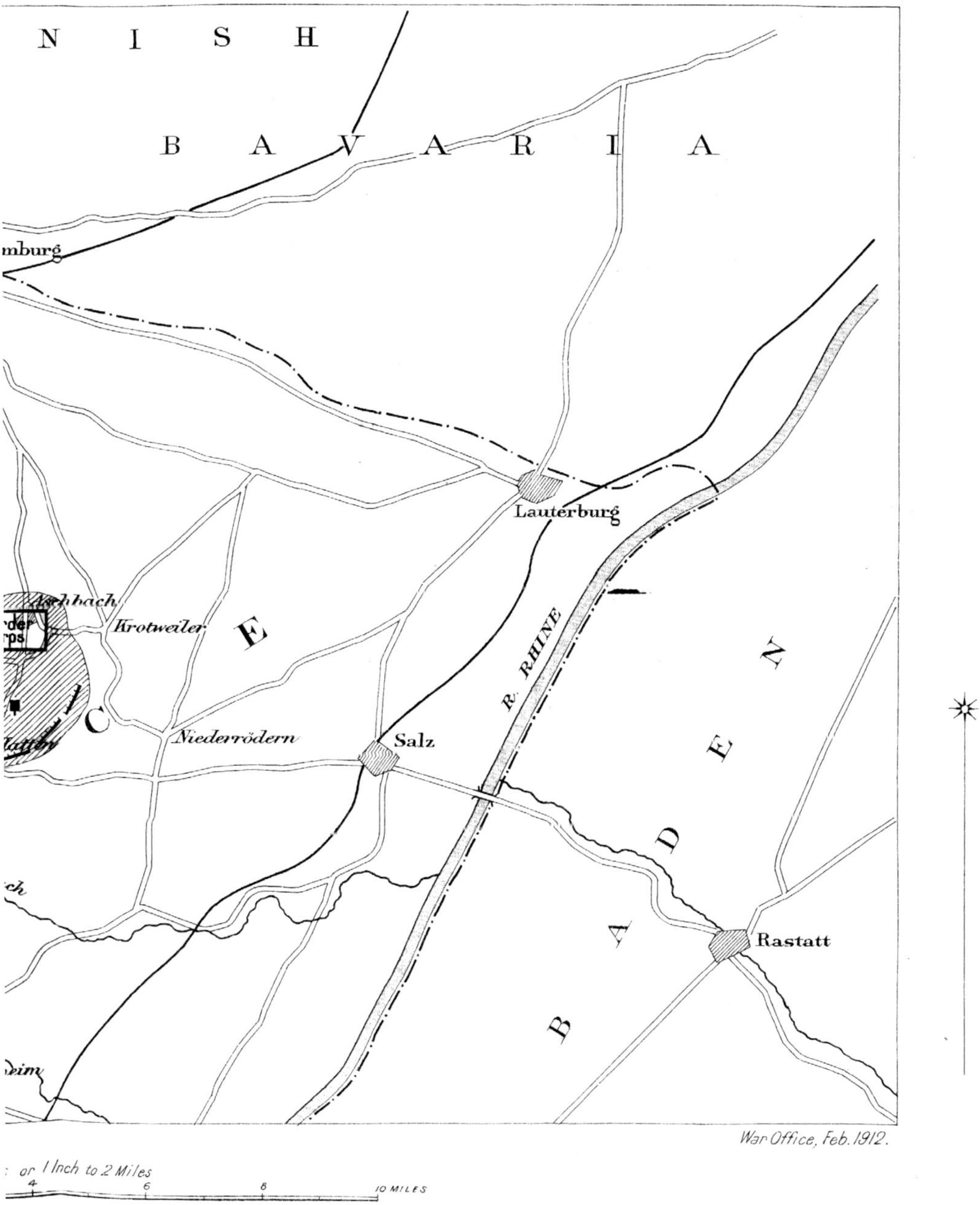

French retreat

The 1st (French) Division and the greater part of the 2nd Division retired on the evening of the 4th August by the Lembach valley, and reached the neighbourhood of Froeschweiler on the morning of the 5th August.

Bonnemain's Cavalry Division joined MacMahon at Froeschweiler about the same time.

Lartigue's Division and Michel's Cavalry Brigade marched on the night of the 4th August from Hagenau to Woerth and Reichshoffen respectively, and arrived at their destinations very early on the 5th.

Raoult's Division was already on the spot, and the infantry of Dumesnil's Division, VIIth Corps, left Colmar and Mulhausen by rail on the night of the 4th–5th August, reaching Reichshoffen on the afternoon and evening of the 5th. The other divisions of the VIIth Corps did not move.

As soon as the news of Weissenburg reached the Emperor he placed the Vth Corps, commanded by General de Failly, under MacMahon's orders. The Marshal at once asked de Failly to send him all available troops on the 6th.

Chapter IV

Woerth

Before entering on an actual description of the ground and the fighting, it is desirable to draw attention to the positions occupied by the two armies,[1] and the considerations that animated the two commanders on the eve of battle.

The position of the French Army in Alsace

The positions of the French Corps on the evening of the 5th August were as follows:–

Ist Corps	At or about Froeschweiler
Ist Division, VIIth Corps	Railed on 5th from Colmar and Mulhausen to Reichshoffen without its artillery
Remainder of VIIth Corps	Mulhausen, Belfort and Lyons
Vth Corps	3rd Division at Bitche
Vth Corps	1st Division 2 miles north of Bitche, after a hard march on the 5th.
Vth Corps	2nd Division Rohrbach and Saargemund, with the enemy menacing in the valley of the Blies.

It is necessary now to consider what action MacMahon should have taken in view of the situation in which he and the troops at his disposal were placed. The general strategical situation has already been discussed in Chapter I, in which it was pointed out that MacMahon's army was virtually a detachment from the main army on the Saar, and was separated from that army by the Vosges Mountains. That being the case it should have conformed to the rules for the employment of a detachment and should have been drawn into the main army, unless it could have been so used as to occupy and draw off from the main theatre a stronger force of the enemy. How then could MacMahon fulfil these conditions? He had in front of him a superior force of the enemy. If he could occupy it in Alsace and prevent it from crossing the Vosges and co-operating with the 1st and IInd German armies in Lorraine, he would be helping his side. But this object could not be achieved by accepting battle against heavy odds. Skilful manoeuvre was necessary, with the double object of drawing the enemy away from the Saar and preserving his own communications.

To carry out such an operation it was necessary that MacMahon should concentrate his available forces, which were still widely dispersed, and obtain accurate information as to the movements of the enemy.

The most important question to decide was the point of concentration. Was there a reasonable prospect of concentration on the Woerth position before he was attacked? Granting that he did not anticipate attack before the 7th, it is more than doubtful whether the still distant portions of the Vth and VIIth Corps could be assembled in that locality in time. Prudence, therefore, dictated the disposition of the troops already assembled in

1 See Map IV.

a suitable manner to effect a retirement if attacked, covered by a strong rearguard, and the selection of an area of concentration further to the south in the direction of Saverne. Such dispositions would have drawn the enemy southwards away from the Saar, would have afforded time for the assembly of an adequate force with which to accept battle with a reasonable prospect of success, and would have directly protected the communications with the main army in Lorraine. The army could have withdrawn through the Vosges at Saverne if it was not considered desirable to fight a battle in Alsace.

The attempt to concentrate on the Woerth position was probably doomed to failure from the start, and was made certain by the reply of de Failly to MacMahon's instructions. De Failly reported that he had only one division ready to move, which he would send to Reichschoffen on the 6th, starting at daybreak. The action of von Seubert's detachment on the Upper Rhine was, moreover, still allowed to hold the remainder of the VIIth Corps far to the south in the neighbourhood of Mulhausen and Belfort.

The value of the Woerth position has already been referred to, and the conclusion arrived at that it depended entirely on its tactical strength. The position was strong against frontal attack, and the left flank was difficult of access, but the right flank was tactically weak, and every prospect of success must disappear if it could not be maintained. It must be admitted, then, that MacMahon had made an injudicious choice of a point of concentration for strategical reasons, and that the position of Woerth offered no compensating advantages from a tactical point of view.

Nor had he decided on a definite course of action if attacked. He did not appreciate the danger of an immediate attack, thinking, as indeed was the case, that the Crown Prince did not intend to advance till the 7th at the earliest. When the action started, he was still in a state of indecision, arguing with Ducrot as to the merits of a certain plan for withdrawing into the Vosges. He first gave the order to retire, and then, his attention being arrested by a fresh outburst of fire, cancelled this order and decided to stay and fight. So the decision to fight a battle on the part of the French commander was arrived at, not on a broad survey of the strategical situation, but, as so often happens in war, on account of a trivial incident which arrested the personal attention of the commander.

Nor had MacMahon done all that was possible to obtain information as to the movements and intentions of the enemy. He had lost touch after Weissenburg, and was ignorant as to the direction in which the bulk of the enemy's forces was moving, whether on Bitche, Woerth, or Strasburg. He was strong in cavalry, but the strategical employment of that arm for the purpose of obtaining information was not at that time understood in the French army, and the conclusion he had arrived at, that he would not be attacked till the 7th, was a pure surmise.

The possible lines of retreat also had not received the attention which they deserved. There were three possible lines of retreat from the Woerth position.

(i) Via Niederbronn and Bitche
(ii) Via Bouxviller to Saverne
(iii) Via Hagenau on Strasburg

If the enemy were to assume the offensive on the Saar MacMahon could not fall back by Bitche as the exits from the passes of the Vosges would be blocked. To fall back on Strasburg would take him away from the Emperor. There remains the road to Saverne, but if this route was to be utilized the imperative necessity of maintaining the right flank is apparent. The Marshal, however, took no steps to do so, the bulk of his cavalry and his reserves being placed in rear of his centre. The maintenance of railway communication with the main army in Lorraine by means of the Strasburg-Bitche-Saargemund line appears to have influenced the Marshal in staying so long at Woerth; but, as has already been shown, an offensive on the part of the enemy north of the Vosges would at once have compromised this line, which was too far forward to be relied on.

Lastly, MacMahon had taken no precautions to make the position which he occupied as secure as possible. Little or no entrenching had been carried out, and only some of the bridges over the Sauer had been destroyed, others being left intact.

History is bound, therefore, to condemn somewhat severely the strategy of the French commander. His position was a difficult one owing to the want of plans and the hesitations of the Emperor's Head Quarters, but he had not done all that was humanly possible to improve matters within the sphere of his own responsibilities.

The position of the IIIrd German Army

On the night of the 5th August the IIIrd German Army was disposed as follows:

IInd Bavarians	Lembach
Vth Corps	Preuschdorf, with outposts on the line Goersdorf – Gunstett in touch with the enemy on the Sauer
XIth Corps	Soultz
Von Werder's Corps	Aschbach
1st Bavarians	Ingolsheim
4th Cavalry Division	Schoenenburg

The army was therefore facing south with three corps in front line, the Vth (Preuschdorf), XIth (Soultz), and Von Werder's (Aschbach), the distance from Preuschdorf to Aschbach being eight miles.[2] The Ist and IInd Bavarians were in second line, but the IInd Bavarians were separated from the rest of the army by the Hochwald, a serious obstacle. The Vth Corps, being the right flank of the front line, was in touch with a superior force of the enemy on the right bank of the Sauer. Up to now the Crown Prince had been doubtful of the direction in which the main French concentration would take place. He had information of French troops at Hagenau and at Bitche, but, on the evening of the 5th August, he concluded, from the information in his possession, that MacMahon would draw in the Vth and VIIth Corps, dispose his troops so as to protect the Hagenau-Saargemund railway, and accept battle behind the Sauer. We are told that his orders for the 6th were based on this assumption. They ran as follows:

> The army will remain concentrated tomorrow round Soultz and execute a change of front.
>
> 1. The IInd Bavarians and Vth Prussian Corps remain in their present position at Lembach and Preuschdorf.
>
> 2. The XIth Prussian Army Corps will wheel to the right and bivouac at Holschloch, its outposts pushed forward towards the Sauer. Surburg and the roads to Hagenau will be occupied.

2 See Map V.

> 3. The Ist Bavarian Corps will advance as far as the neighbourhood of Lobsann and Lampertsloch. Outposts thrown forward through the Hochwald in the direction of the Sauer.
> 4. The 4th Cavalry Division remains in bivouac, but will front westward.
> 5. Werder's Corps will march to Reimersweiler and show front towards the south, its outposts pushed forward towards the Hagenau forest. The roads to Kuhlendorf and the railway at Hoffen are to be protected by strong outpost detachments.
> The headquarters remain at Soultz."

One or two points in connexion with these dispositions are worthy of comment. Two corps and the cavalry division remained stationary, and the remaining corps each moved a distance of six miles. Moreover, no corps was at a greater distance than fifteen miles from the Sauer on the evening of the 5th, and the greater part of the army was within ten miles. The considerations that should have influenced MacMahon as to remaining to fight a battle on the Sauer have already been discussed, and the arguments against such a course have been stated. The Crown Prince's information seems to have been accurate, but his conclusions hardly seem to have been justified. Time is the essence of strategy, and an opportunity lost may not recur. To waste a day in minor adjustments in the positions of his corps might well have afforded his adversary an opportunity of escaping from an awkward situation. The corps were all within supporting distance of one another, and with care in the allotment of roads in the Army Orders they could have been brought to the field earlier than was actually the case. The XIth Corps, for instance, marched by a single road, which was not necessary, and the arrangements made for the march of the other corps are open to considerable criticism.

The Crown Prince was anxious about the exposed position of the Vth Corps, and his anxiety led him to commit a blunder. On the afternoon of the 5th he sent an order to the IInd Bavarians to direct their attention to the Bitche road and to Langensultzbach.

> Should the report of cannon be heard on the following morning in the direction of Woerth, a division of the corps was to advance against the enemy's left flank, the remainder to be halted facing Bitche.[3]

This order was not repeated to the Vth Corps, with results that we shall see presently. But what justification was there for the Crown Prince's anxiety? The Dieffenbach ridge, which was held by the Vth Corps' outposts, was a strong position, and surely he could have wished for no better solution than that the French should attack him in that position. The distances that his corps would have to march to reach the field would be much reduced and the issue could not be doubtful.

The battlefield

The position occupied by the French at Woerth was on a spur of the Vosges running in a southerly direction into the Rhine plain. The root of the spur is at Neehweiler, and the apex at Morsbronn, the distance between the two being about 4½ miles. Facing the Woerth position to the east, and separated from it by the valley of the Sauer, is the Dieffenbach ridge, extending from the wooded Hochwald to the village of Gunstett, where it drops

3 *German Official History.*

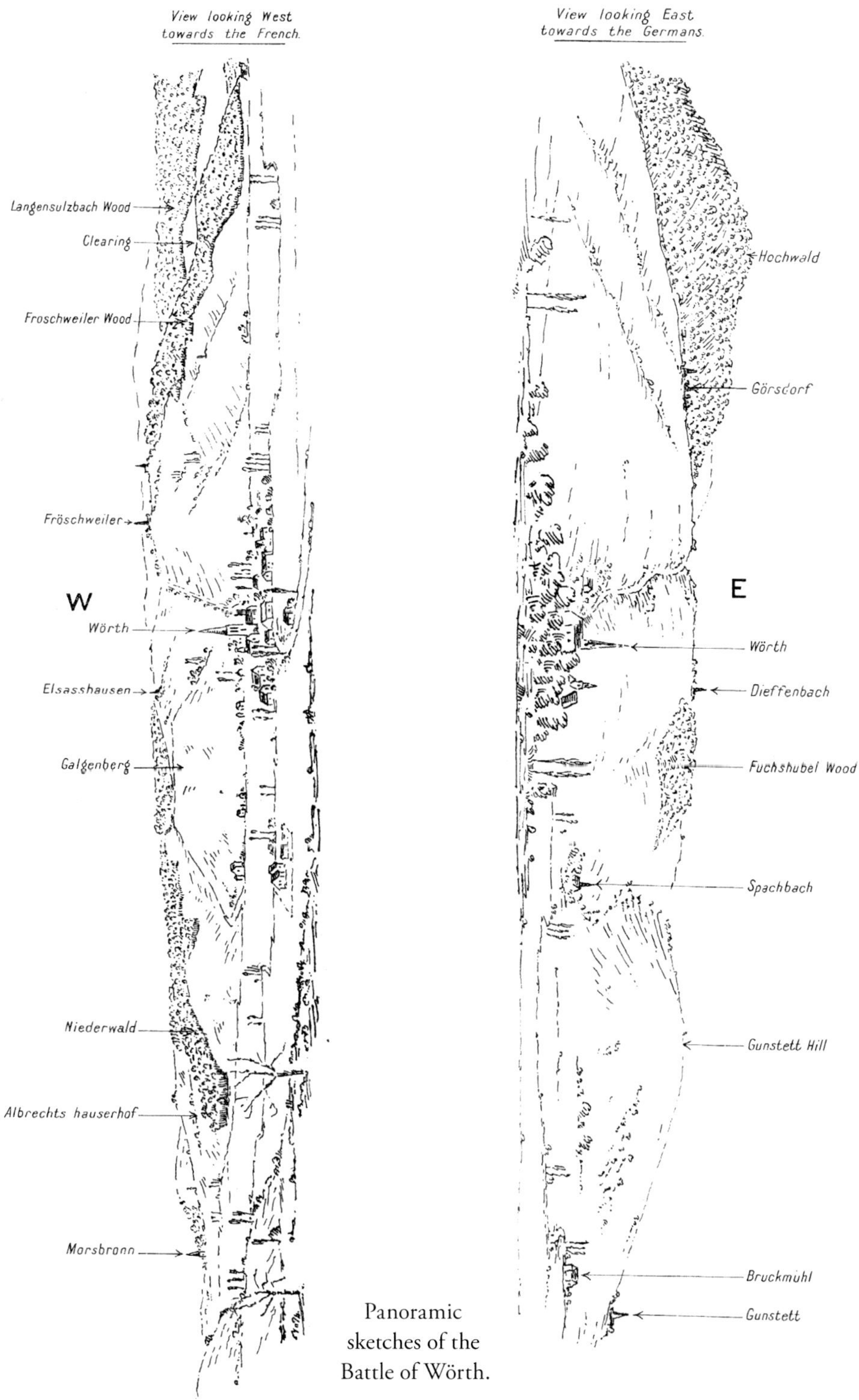

Panoramic sketches of the Battle of Wörth.

DISPOSITION OF THE FRENCH TROOP
6TH AUGUST 1870.

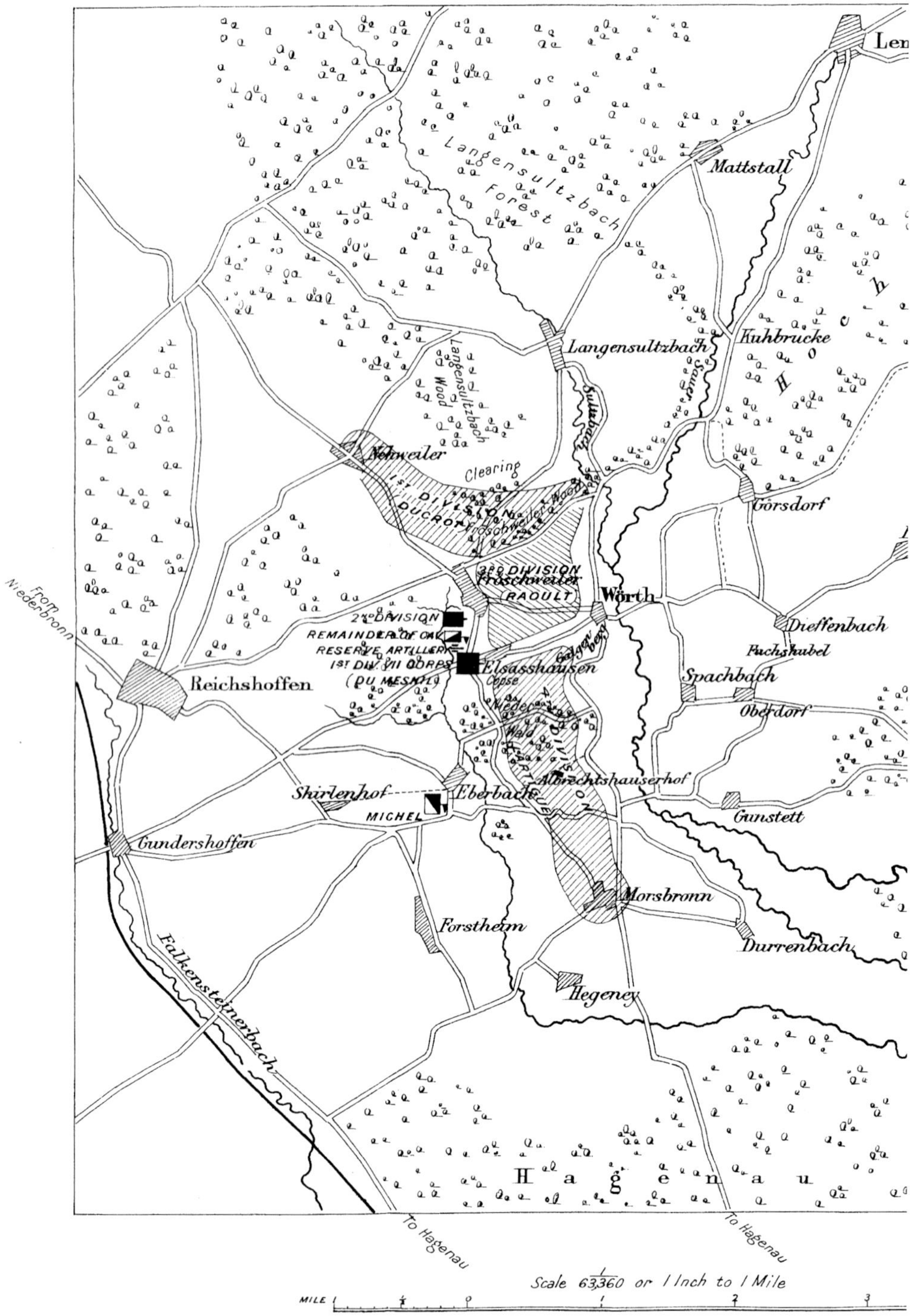

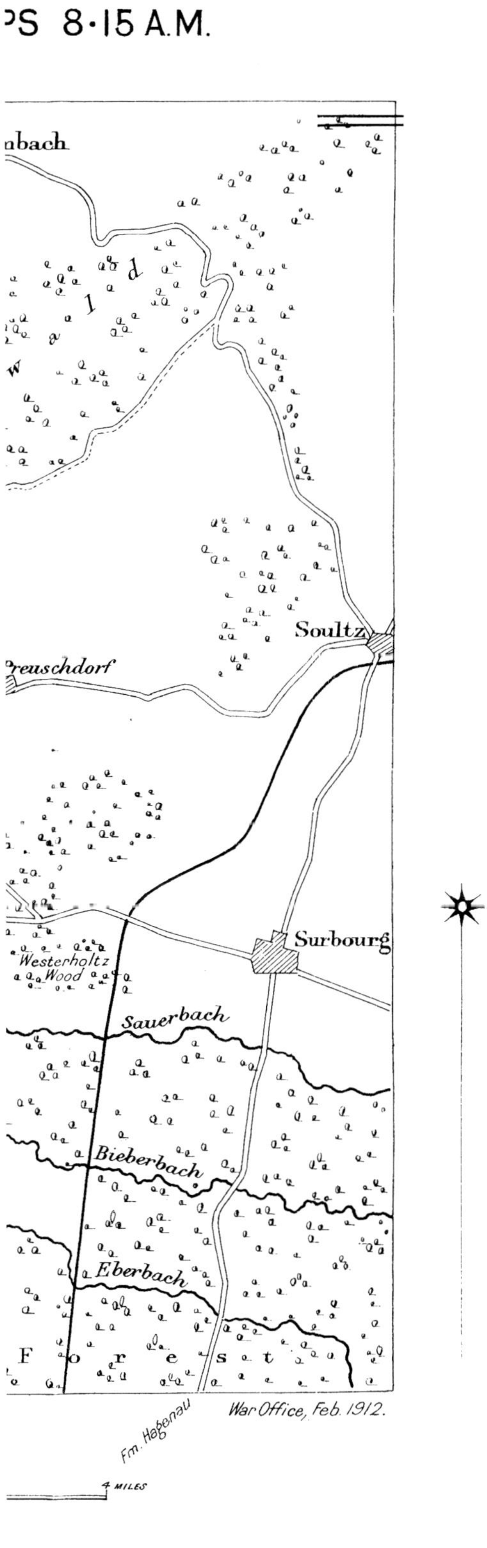
PS 8·15 A.M.
nbach
Soultz
Preuschdorf
Surbourg
Westerholtz Wood
Sauerbach
Bieberbach
Eberbach
F o r e s t
Fm. Hagenau
War Office, Feb. 1912.
4 MILES

Map VI

somewhat abruptly into the plain. The Sauer is a stream 30 to 40 feet wide, rising in the Vosges, and running through a flat valley of meadow land of an average width of some 800 yards. On the day of the battle, the stream was from 4 to 8 feet deep, being much swollen by floods. The Hochwald, forest clad and rising to a height of 1,500 feet, is a serious tactical obstacle and completely cuts off the Dieffenbach ridge from the Lembach valley. The chief tactical points on the Woerth position are the villages and woods and the spurs running down into the valley of the Sauer. The principal villages are Neehweiler, Froeschweiler, Woerth, Elsasshausen, and Morsbronn, to which must be added the farm called the Albrechtshauserhof just south of the Niederwald. The important woods are the Langensultzbach wood, the Froeschweiler wood, the Elsasshausen copse, and the Niederwald, mostly beech woods without much dense undergrowth. Apart from the Morsbronn spur, which is a very distinctive feature, the most important spurs are the Galgenberg, running east from Elsasshausen, and the spur running from Froeschweiler to a point just north-west of the village of Woerth. No account of the ground would be complete without mentioning the narrow clearing between the Langensultzbach wood and the Froeschweiler wood, the wooded spur between the Sultzbach and the Sauer, and the peculiar dome-shaped Gunstett hill, which is separated from the main Dieffenbach ridge by a big re-entrant, at the mouth of which lies the village of Spachbach. A last reference must be made to the Forstheim ridge, which lies to the west of the Morsbronn ridge, and is separated from it by the little valley of the Eberbach.

Such ground as is not wooded is much cultivated with hop gardens, vineyards, and corn. There are many terraces and sunken roads, and the terrain on the position itself is unsuitable for cavalry, which arm, however, could have found plenty of scope for its activities in the Rhine plain.

French dispositions

The French dispositions at 8.15 a.m., when they had taken post for battle, are shown on Map VI.

The troops available consisted of:

	{ 1st Division	Ducrot
Ist Corps	{ 2nd Division	Pellé
	{ 3rd Division	Raoult
	{ 4th Division	Lartigue
VIIth Corps	1st Division	Du Mesnil (less its artillery).
Bonnemain's Cavalry Division.		
Duhesme's Cavalry Division		
Reserve Artillery – 8 batteries.		

The strength of the divisions varied considerably, but the total is given as 46,000 combatants, consisting of 58 battalions, 44 squadrons, 107 guns and 24 machine guns.

The troops were disposed in the following order:

Ducrot	Neehweiler to southern edge of Froeschweiler wood.
Raoult	Southern, edge of Froeschweiler wood to Elsasshausen (exclusive).
Du Mesnil	About Elsasshausen.
Lartigue	Elsasshausen copse to Morsbronn.

Michel's Cuirassier Brigade	Eberbach.
Pellé	}
Remainder of Cavalry	} Under cover between Froeschweiler and Reserve
Artillery	} Elsasshausen

There are two prominent salients in the position – the Froeschweiler wood and the Niederwald. These were held by the front line, which in other parts of the position was placed well down the forward slopes of the spurs. The second line ran along the crest of the ridge. The divisional artillery, which consisted of two batteries of 9-pr. or 25-pr. guns and 1 battery of machine guns in each division, was distributed throughout the front. Within reach of the field were approximately 100,000 Germans, consisting of 100 battalions, 80 squadrons, and 360 guns.

Chapter V

The Battle of Woerth

It is not proposed to give a detailed account of, the fighting, for which the reader is referred to the French and German Official Histories, but an attempt will be made to bring out the salient points in the different phases of the battle, namely, the engagement of the advanced guards, the general engagement, and the decisive attack.

The engagement of the advanced guards

The outposts of the Vth Corps were found by the 20th Brigade, 2 squadrons of cavalry, and 1 battery, under General Von Walther. They were disposed as follows:–

½ Battn. 37th Regt Goersdorf } Furnishing outposts on line of the
1 Battn. 50th Regt Dieffenbach } Sauer with 1 Company at the
1 Battn 50th Regt Gunstett } Bruchmill.
1 Squadron Gunstett }

Remainder of outpost troops near Dieffenbach. Woerth was not occupied.

At 4 a.m., Von Walther heard a commotion in the village of Woerth, which he took to be caused by the enemy retiring. It was very misty and had been raining hard. Von Walther sent to General Von Kirchbach, the Commander of the Vth Corps, and asked for leave to reconnoitre and see what the enemy was doing. By 7 a.m., the mist had cleared, but as no answer had been received from Von Kirchbach, Von Walther took upon himself to employ 1 battalion in reconnoitring. He brought his battery into action near Dieffenbach, and the battalion advanced towards Woerth. The battery fired a few rounds into the village, on which a few French soldiers, who had left their bivouacs in search of food and drink, cleared off. The Germans entered the village, found the bridge destroyed, waded the stream, and a section pushed on to the Western outskirts of the village. When they reached this point they were fired on by a battery of French Artillery, and a little artillery engagement ensued with Von Walther's battery near Dieffenbach. As it was clear that the French had not retired, Von Walther withdrew his reconnaissance, leaving a company in Woerth.

At about the same time that this was occurring, General Lartigue decided to push a reconnaissance towards Gunstett with the object of ascertaining if the Germans were in strength in that neighbourhood. He ordered a battalion of the 1st Chasseurs, supported by a field battery, a machine gun battery, and the Zouaves in occupation of the Eastern edge of the Niederwald, to turn the German outpost out of the Bruchmill, and to occupy Gunstett Hill. The French advanced just as the advanced guard of the XIth Corps was approaching Gunstett from the East. It will be remembered that this Corps, in accordance with the Crown Prince's orders, was to march on the morning of the 6th to Holschloch and Surburg, and place outposts towards the Sauer. When the French advanced, the outposts were just taking up their position on the Western edge of the Westerholtz wood. The French were met by the battalion of the 50th Regiment in Gunstett, which was at once supported by a battalion of the advanced guard of the XIth Corps. They did not get beyond the line of the Hagenau high road, where, for the time being, we must leave them.

When General Von Hartmann, Commanding the IInd Bavarians, received on the afternoon of the 6th the instructions from the Crown Prince that have already been referred to, he ordered the 4th Division of his Corps to, push forward to Mattstall at daybreak on the 6th, and establish an outpost at the Kuhbrucke in order that might be able to communicate with the Vth Corps by the road running round the western end of the Hochwald. When on the morning of the 6th he heard artillery fire to the South, he at once ordered the 4th Division to advance towards Froeschweiler. At about 9 a.m., the 7th Bavarian Brigade advanced through Langensultzbach, and mistaking its direction, moved through the forest on Nechweiler, instead of Froeschweilei. The 8th Brigade advanced simultaneously on its left and kept the right direction, the result being that while the 7th Brigade was moving west on Neehweiler, the 8th Brigade very soon became engaged with the 2nd Turcos, who were holding the north-eastern corner of the Froeschweiler wood. The 7th Brigade, hearing firing to their left rear, changed direction to the left, and presently arrived in some disorder at the south-west corner of the Langensultzbach wood. They then endeavoured to form a firing line on the southern edge of the wood, but the units became much mixed up in the process. At the moment the northern edge of the Froeschweiler wood was not occupied by the French, except at the north-east corner held by the 2nd Turcos. Although the 7th Bavarian Brigade had no enemy in front of them, they did not advance across the clearing at once, but contented themselves with keeping up a hot fire on the northern edge of the Froeschweiler wood. Very soon the French extended portions of the 96th and 48th Regiments to oppose them. The Bavarians then made repeated attempts to cross the clearing. They reinforced their firing line till 10 Battalions were hotly engaged between the south-west corner of the Langensultzbach wood and the sawmill. They attempted to bring up two batteries in support to a spur which runs from the south-eastern edge of the Langensultzbach wood to the sawmill, but the French fire was so hot that the guns could not get into action. All attempts to cross the clearing failed. At 10 a.m., 1½ battalions of the 1st Zouaves counter-attacked the right flank of the Bavarians, and drove them through the wood and across the Sager. According to the German Official History: "A Prussian Orderly Officer[1] brought verbal instructions to General Von Hartmann at 10.30 a.m. to suspend the contest." It is clear, however, that the original withdrawal was due to the vigour of the French counterstroke, and not to any order from superior authority. The effect was such that for practical purposes the 4th Bavarian Division was deprived of offensive power for the remainder of the day. The Zouaves returned to their original position, and Von Hartmann rallied his men and got clear by 11.30 a.m. Just about this time, he received a request from Von Kirchbach to support him, but all he was-able to do in response was to undertake to hold his ground and arrest the further withdrawal of his troops.

We must now turn again to the Vth Corps. As soon as Von Walther got his reconnaissance clear in the centre it became evident that engagements were springing up on both flanks. General Von Esch, the Chief General Staff Officer of the Vth Corps, had ridden forward with an order to cease fire, but on becoming aware of the situation

1 The "French Official History" gives this officer's name as Lieutenant Lauterbach, Adjutant of Brigade to General von Walther, but states than he left his General at 8.45 a.m., and did not reach Langensultzbach till 10.30 a,m., when he met General von Hartmann.

he decided, in consultation with the General Officer Commanding 10th Division, that it would never do in the circumstances to break off the engagement entirely in the centre. An order was accordingly sent to the artillery of the, corps to move forward and come into action, and the corps was ordered to get under arms. As has already been stated, it had been raining heavily, and the country on either side of the Dieffenbach-Woerth road being arable land was consequently very heavy going. The guns trotted down the road in column of route and, when about half way down the slope, turned off on either hand. It took some 45 minutes for the 84 guns to get into action. The French in reply reinforced the Divisional Artillery, already in action in the centre of the position, with 6 batteries of the Reserve Artillery, but the French guns were dispersed while the German guns were massed in one long line.[2]

An artillery duel ensued, in which the German Artillery very soon showed its superiority. The French Artillery withdrew from this unequal contest after about 40 minutes. They had suffered, but not very heavily, and had been in no sense destroyed. Their withdrawal seems to have been due to the fact that they realized that they were not doing much good, and as the Commander of the Artillery thought that the Ammunition Park had not arrived he was afraid of running short of ammunition.[3] From this time forward, though the French Artillery were frequently able to intermit in the action, and often with effect, the German Artillery so completely dominated the situation in this part of the field that the interventions of the French Artillery never assumed a threatening aspect, and the German Artillery were able to devote the greater part of their attention to the support of their own infantry, and to repelling counter-attacks. Such, moreover, was the confidence which the superiority of the German Artillery inspired, that Von Kirchbach at a later stage was able to use up his infantry to the last man, being fully satisfied that the strength of his artillery made his front inviolable, and that there was no danger of a French offensive penetrating the German centre.

While the artillery were deploying, Von Kirchbach arrived on the field. It must be borne in mind that, at this moment, heavy fighting was taking place on both flanks, so he decided to "occupy Woerth and the heights beyond" with one brigade. Various motives have been attributed to Von Kirchbach for arriving at this decision. He is stated to have been influenced by the situation on the flanks, fearing that if he remained inactive the French might mass reserves against either flank or both, with the result that a portion or portions of the army might experience a severe repulse. He is further said to have desired to establish himself on the right bank of the Sauer so as to be able to cover the passage of the main body of the corps over the river. Again, he is said to have desired to force the enemy's infantry to disclose their position and subject themselves to the fire of his superior artillery. Whatever may have been actually in his mind at the time, he issued orders at 10 a.m. for the 20th Brigade to move forward in two columns

2¼ Battalions 37th Regiment via Woerth.

2 Battalions 50th Regiment via Spachbach.

2 The German guns fired common shell with percussion fuzes only, and many of their shells buried themselves in the soft ground and did not burst. The French Artillery was equipped with common and shrapnel shell in the proportion of 6 of the former to 1 of the latter. They also carried some case shot. They used only time fuzes, which, for the common shell, could be burst at 1,500 and 2,800 yards, and for the shrapnel could be used at four ranges between 550 and 1,450 yards.

3 The Ammunition Park had arrived at Reichshoffen the previous evening, but its Commander had not reported the fact to the Commander of the Reserve Artillery.

He also informed the Commanders of the IInd Bavarians and the XIth Corps of his intentions, and asked for their support. The troops moved forward at 11 a.m. and crossed the Sauer by improvised bridges made of hop poles. Some were drowned, and some casualties were suffered during the passage of the river from the fire of the French skirmishers. After crossing the river the two columns converged towards the Galgenberg, but, as they started at the same time, and had different distances to go, the two attacks were not simultaneous. The flank of the left column was fired on from the Niederwald, and a portion of the troops were drawn in that direction. The Hagenau high road was crossed, and some progress was made up the slopes of the Galgenberg, when the 2nd Zouaves counterattacked. The Zouaves were supported by portions of the 36th Regiment, 21st and 17th Chasseurs, and they drove the 50th Regiment back to the high road and the 37th Regiment into Woerth. They followed up into the village, but were driven out and suffered severely from artillery fire in retiring. This counter-attack drew in the whole of the 19th Brigade to support the 20th Brigade.

We left the advanced guard of the XIth Corps engaged with the French troops sent by Lartigue to drive the enemy out of the Bruchmill. The 41st Brigade and 4 batteries moved forward to reinforce the 2 battalions already engaged. The original object of this advance appears to have been to secure a defensive position on the left bank of the Sauer. Two columns were hastily formed and advanced as under:

1 battalion 87th Regiment }
2 companies 87th Regiment } via Spachbach.
1 battalion 80th Regiment }
1 battalion 87th Regiment }
2 companies 87th Regiment } via Gunstett.
1 battalion 80th Regiment }

The haste in forming these two columns was no doubt responsible for the breaking up of the regimental organization, but it resulted in the loss of tactical unity in the XIth Corps from the very start of the action, and bore fruit later.

The Spachbach column became engaged with the enemy, and the initiative of the regimental officers appears to have led first of all to the passage of the river, and subsequently to the attack of the Niederwald. Owing to the exposure of the eastern edge of the wood to artillery fire from Gunstett Hill, the Germans had little difficulty in driving the 3rd Zouaves back from the edge of the wood and in entering it. Once inside the wood they became engaged in a desperate fight with the Zouaves, and were deprived of artillery support. The Zouaves counter-attacked and drove them back over the river, but did not follow up owing to the enemy's artillery fire.

The Gunstett column crossed at about the same time and advanced against the 1st Chasseurs, who were holding the line of the high road. The Chasseurs at first fell back, but turned about when reinforced by a battalion and 2 companies of the 3rd Turcos and supported by 2 battalions 56th Regiment, and counter-attacking the Germans in front and flank drove them back over the river in spite of the fire of the 4 batteries on Gunstett Hill. The Turcos followed up to the outskirts of the village of Gunstett, and when compelled to retire, held on obstinately in a hop garden near the bridge. The 56th Regiment assisted the Turcos to withdraw, and this counter-attack drew in 5 battalions of the 42nd Brigade to support the advanced guard of the XIth Corps.

The advanced guards of the Vth and XIth Prussian Corps and the 4th Division, IInd Bavarians, had thus made isolated and disjointed attacks on the French position, and by 11.30 a.m. they had been repulsed everywhere. 17,000 men had been engaged, and the losses had been heavy. The only troops that had gained a footing on the right bank of the Sauer were those belonging to the Vth Corps which were holding Woerth, and were hanging on by their eyelids, so to speak, on the line of the high road at the foot of the Galgenberg.

The General engagement

It is necessary now to hark back for a moment to an important event which took place an hour previously, viz., at 10.30 a.m. The Crown Prince, as has been stated, was at Soultz. When the firing was heard early in the morning he sent an officer of the Headquarter Staff to the Headquarters of the Vth Corps to report. This officer's report left the field at 9.30 a.m., and gave the state of affairs as far as it could be seen from the Dieffenbach ridge. At 10.30 a.m. Von Kirchbach received a message from the Crown Prince, which ran as follows: – "Do not continue the struggle, and avoid everything that may induce a fresh one."[4] The receipt of this message placed Von Kirchbach in a difficult position. The situation had changed considerably since the officer wrote the report on which the Crown Prince's order was based, and the Crown Prince, when he caused the order to be sent, was not aware of the situation which now confronted Von Kirchbach. It, therefore, became the duty of the latter to act on his own responsibility, and to ignore the Crown Prince's order if he thought it advisable to do so.

Basing his opinion on the loss of *moral* that would result if an action that had proceeded so far with so little success should be broken off, he decided to continue the action, and called upon Von Hartmann (IInd Bavarians) and Von Bose (XIth Corps) to support him. The IInd Bavarians, as we have already noted, were in no position to render assistance.

We must now turn again to the XIth Corps. General Von Bose, Commanding XIth Corps, was distant from the field when he received Von Kirchbach's first appeal for assistance. He replied that his orders precluded his engaging his corps, but he rode forward at once to Gunstett Hill, and on arrival there received another urgent appeal for support. To this second appeal he replied that he would not leave the Vth Corps in the lurch, and at once prepared to bring the full strength of his corps into play.

We have already seen how the greater part of the 41st and 42nd Brigades composing the 21st Division of the XIth Corps had been drawn into the fight to support the advanced guard against the French counter-attacks. The intention of Von Bose appears to have been to attack the enemy in front via Spachbach and Gunstett with the 21st Division, and to assign to the 22nd Division the task of attacking the enemy's right flank. That there was confusion in assigning the troops to their various tasks seems to be proved without question, and may be attributed to two main causes, namely, the haste with which the columns were formed, and the abuse of initiative on the part of General Von Schkopp, Commanding the 44th Brigade. General Von Gersdorff, Commanding the 22nd Division, allotted to the 43rd Brigade the task of attacking the French right, ordering 2 battalions 32nd Regiment to move via Durrenbach on Morsbronn, and 2 battalions 95th Regiment "to move up to the fighting line of the 21st Division." He also sent an order to the 44th Brigade to move to Gunstett in reserve. Von Schkopp had, however, diverted the march

4 This order was repeated to the Commanders of the IInd Bavarians and. the XIth Corps.

of the 44th Brigade by a by-path as soon as the head of the Brigade emerged from the Westerholtz wood, and when he received the order from his chief he was already well on his way to Durrenbach. He took upon himself not to comply with the order, but sending to Gunstett only his rear Regiment, the 83rd, he placed himself at the head of the 32nd and 94th Regiments, and continued to move on Morsbronn. It thus arose that the force moving on Morsbronn, instead of consisting of 2 battalions only, as would have been the case if the orders of Von Gersdorff had been carried out, now consisted of 2 battalions 32nd Regiment and 3 battalions 94th Regiment, a formidable force. While, therefore, the breaking up of formations was aggravated by Von Schkopp's action, the immediate success of the turning movement must be directly attributed to his indiscipline and abuse of initiative. Such is the fortune of war.

In the end, then, 3 columns of attack were formed as follows:

Moving by Spachbach – objective the Niederwald:

3 battalions, 88th Regiment (42nd Brigade)
1½ battalions 80th Regiment (41st Brigade)
1½ battalions 80th Regiment (41st Brigade)

Moving by Gunstett – objective the Albrechtshauserhof:

2 battalions, 95th Regiment (43rd Brigade)
1½ battalions 87th Regiment (41st Brigade)
1 battalion 80th Regiments (41st Brigade)
1 rifle battalion (21st Division)

Moving by Durrenbach – objective Morsbronn:

2 battalions, 32nd Regiment (43rd Brigade)
2 battalions 94th Regiment (44th Brigade)
2 companies 80th Regiment (41st Bridgade)

The whole of the artillery of the corps was ordered to Gunstett Hill, where 72 guns cane into action at reduced intervals, 2 batteries being crowded out.

The Reserve of the Corps was assembled East of Gunstett, and consisted of:

82nd Regiment (42nd Brigade)
1 battalion, 95th Regiment (43rd Brigade)
83rd Regiment (44th Brigade)

It will thus be seen that there were portions of the 80th Regiment in all three Columns, and that no single Brigade remained intact. The organization of the Corps was completely broken up, and the subordinate Commanders can have had no clearly-defined duties.

The frontal attack, having the shortest distance to go, got to work first, and fully occupied the attention of the French. As in the case of the Vth Corps, the great massed battery on Gunstett Hill very, soon dominated the situation. Lartigue's weak divisional artillery was not reinforced from the Reserve Artillery, although the artillery positions available on the Morsbronn ridge were probably superior to the German positions on Gunstett Hill. The French batteries were shortly obliged to withdraw to positions that were defiladed from Gunstett Hill, and consequently were unable to oppose the advance of the German infantry with effect. The frontal attack, therefore, continued to gain ground, and to press back the infantry of Lartigue's Division till possession was gained of the Abrechtshauserhof.

Morsbronn, was held by an outpost of two companies only, which gave way before the turning movement of the Durrenbach column. The Germans occupied the village

BATTLE OF WÖRTH

SITUATION AT 11a.m.

6TH AUGUST 1870

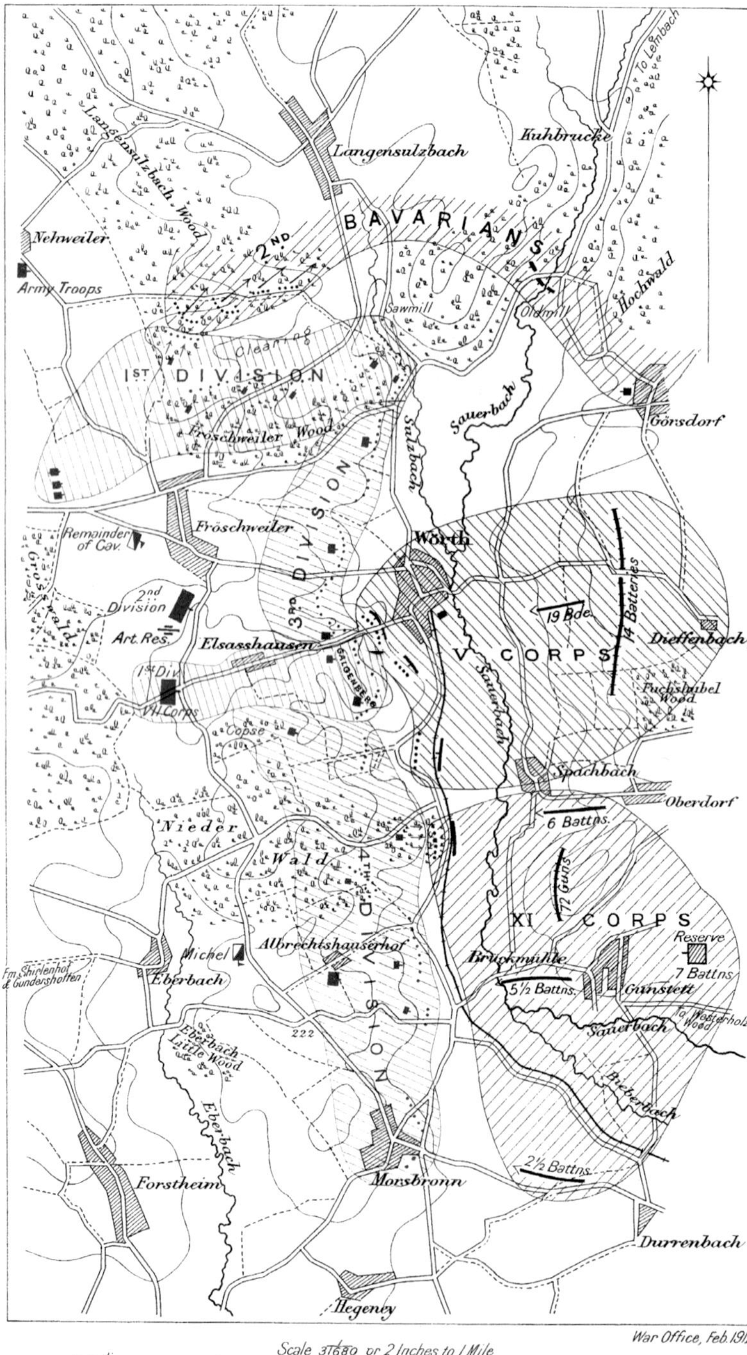

War Office, Feb. 1912

Map VII

and advanced up the slopes. The position of Lartigue's infantry now became critical. They were driven into a somewhat confined space, forced to face two ways at once, and subjected to the fire of a greatly superior artillery. The turning movement had thrown Lartigue's right back across the ridge in a line composed of a confused mass of men of the 56th Regiment, 3rd Turcos, and 1st Chasseurs. The artillery endeavoured to co-operate from a position, in rear of the crest defiladed from Gunstett Hill, but their efforts were not very successful. The Albrechtshauserhof was in possession of the enemy, and strong bodies of German infantry were pressing forward on all sides. In his extremity, Lartigue appealed to MacMahon for reinforcements, but received the reply that the Marshal had none to send to him, and that he must stand firm. MacMahon added that a Division of the Vth Corps had left Bitche at 4 a.m., and that he hoped it would arrive in time. Lartigue foresaw that his Division would be annihilated if he persisted, so he endeavoured to extricate the debris of his force. He sent his guns to a position north-west of Eberbach on the Forstheim ridge to cover the retirement, he got together some men of mixed units, made a counter-attack towards the Albrechtshauserhof, and asked General Michel, commanding the Cuirassier Brigade, to help him by charging the enemy approaching from the direction of Morsbronn with a regiment of Cuirassiers.

General Michel at first demurred, but being again appealed to he consented. His brigade at this time was under cover on the left bank of the Eberbach, just east of the village of that name. It was facing east in three lines thus:

4 squadrons, 8th Cuirassiers
3 squadrons 9th Cuirassiers
2 squadrons 6th Lancers.

There were no scouts out, and the ground had not been reconnoitred with a view to its possibilities for cavalry action. It was most unsuitable for the shock action of cavalry, being much intersected with vineyards, hop gardens, little banks and ditches, cultivation, and sunken roads. Michel asked Lartigue what he was to charge, and the latter pointed to the German infantry advancing from Morsbronn. The 8th Cuirassiers in front line found the ground so cramped that they were forced on to a front of two squadrons. As they advanced, their left was fired on at close range, but though they lost heavily they continued their career towards Morsbronn. The German infantry opened out in front of them, took refuge in the hop gardens and behind cover as they went by, and fired into their flanks. They reached the north-east corner of the village and charged down the street, fired at from the houses. At the end of the street they found a barricade, so had to turn about and try and find another loophole of escape. Eventually, about 50 men found their way into the plain and galloped on towards Durrenbach and the Hagenau forest till their horses were exhausted. The remainder were either killed or taken prisoners.

The 9th Cuirassiers charged in second line to the right of the line taken by the 8th Cuirassiers, and were followed by the 6th Lancers. They were able to deploy into line, and galloped over two companies of the 32nd Regiment which formed the extreme left of Von Schkopp's infantry. The greater part of these two regiments then made for the south-west corner of Morsbronn, and rode into the main village street which runs east and west. The houses were occupied by the German infantry, and the exits from the village were by now all barricaded. Few of the cavalry escaped. The dead horses lay so thickly in the street that later in the day the Germans were obliged to abandon the attempt to get their transport wagons through the village.

The remnants of the cavalry endeavouring to rejoin found themselves cut off, and many were taken prisoners. A curious incident is related in the French Official History. A remnant of about 50 Cuirassiers were returning to the west of Morsbronn up the Eberbach valley, when they were espied by a squadron of the 13th Hussars. The Hussars advanced to attack, but the Cuirassiers wheeled about, and the two forces approached within ten yards of one another and halted. There was no charge, but a few men on either side drew their pistols, and a few saddles were emptied. Both the combatants then withdrew, leaving one another unmolested. The German Official History describes this incident as a "bloody collision."

This disastrous charge, combined with the counter-attack of some groups of men belonging to the 56th Regiment, 3rd Turcos, 1st Chasseurs, and 3rd Zouaves, gained a little respite for Lartigue's infantry, which he was able to withdraw towards Shirlenhoff and Gundershoffen, covered by parties in the wood and, village of Eberbach.

One regiment of the XIth Corps followed Lartigue's division for a short distance only. The remainder, supported by, the greater part of the reserve's of the corps, plunged into the Niederwald, where they fought desperately with the 3rd Zouaves, who disputed every inch of the ground. They did not reach the northern edge of the wood till 2 p.m., by which time the corps was in a state of inextricable confusion. All tactical unity and control was lost, and, for the time being, the troops were incapable of a. further offensive effort.

The Crown Prince arrived on the field about mid-day and was evidently at sea for some little time as to the state of affairs. His first inclination was to order all available troops to move towards the centre, probably being impressed with what he considered to be the dangerous position of the Vth Corps. The first order issued by Count Von Blumenthal, Chief of the Staff to the Crown Prince, was as follows:

> 6th August, 1 p.m.
>
> The Vth Corps will postpone its attack till the approach of General Von der Tann, who has been directed to the north of Preuschdorf. The approach of the 21st Division, which has been ordered to march on Woerth, will also be awaited. They cannot arrive for an hour or two. Werder's Corps has also been ordered up, but it will be quite 3 hours before it arrives.
>
> (Signed) Von Blumenthal

As we have already seen, the 21st Division was fully engaged with Lartigue's Division at this time. Different counsels appear to have prevailed shortly, for the German Official History tells us that the Crown Prince judged that even if MacMahon had succeeded in concentrating a division of the Vth Corps with his own troops, the French forces opposed to him could not exceed 60,000 men. Although portions of his own army were still at a distance from the field, they could all arrive during the afternoon. A better opportunity might not occur, so he decided to press the battle to a conclusion. The Crown Prince accordingly issued the following order at 1 p.m:

> The IInd Bavarian Corps will press upon the left flank of the enemy in such a manner as to gain a position in rear of it towards ·Reichshoffen.

> The Ist Bavarian Corps will march as rapidly as possible and come into line between the IInd Bavarians and the Vth Corps, holding a division in reserve.
>
> The XIth Corps will advance with energy via Elsasshausen and past the Niederwald on Froeschweiler.
>
> Of Werder's Corps the Wurtemburg Division will follow the XIth Corps on Gunstett and over the Sauer; the Baden Division will move for the present as far as Surburg.

No mention is made in the German Official History of the 4th Cavalry Division, but according to Von Hahnke, it was to form the General Reserve of the army.

The fight, in the centre of the field, remained stationary for some little time. At 2 p.m., however, the XIth Corps appeared to be making good progress on the left, so a further offensive effort was made by the Vth Corps.

> 2 battalions, 17th Brigade, attacked from Woerth with their right on the Froeschweiler-Woerth road.
>
> 2 battalions, 18th Brigade, crossed at Spachbach and attacked the southern end of the Galgenberg.

The 17th Brigade was counter-attacked by the 2nd Zouaves and driven back to Woerth, while the 18th Brigade was counter-attacked by portions of the 2nd Zouaves, 21st Regiment, and 17th Chasseurs, and driven back to the river. But the counter-attacking troops suffered heavily when withdrawing.

Four battalions of the Ist Bavarians arrived at Goersdorf at 1 p.m., and at 2 p.m. the leading brigade crossed the Sauer at the Old Mill and advanced over the wooded spur, which here fills the angle between the Sauer and the Sultzbach, to attack the defenders of the Froeschweiler wood. This attack could make no progress, possibly to some extent owing to the absence of artillery support, and it was found necessary to order the other brigade of the Ist Bavarians to cross the spur, so as to gain the valley of the Sultzbach and attack the left of the 2nd Turcos, who were defending the wood most stubbornly. No ground was gained in this direction up to 3 p.m.

At 2.30 p.m. Von Kirchbach ordered a general offensive of what remained of the Vth Corps. The 17th and 19th Brigades attacked from Woerth, and the 18th and 20th Brigades from Spachbach. Ground was now gained in this part of the field. The crest of the Galgenberg was reached, the defenders being driven back towards Elsasshausen. The Woerth column also penetrated up the big re-entrant towards Froeschweiler. These successes disturbed the equanimity of MacMahon more than those of the XIth Corps, possibly because they came more immediately under his observation. He consequently ordered a succession of counterattacks, which were delivered with great vigour. The 3rd Regiment, moving south of Elsasshausen, counter-attacked towards the Galgenberg and drove the Germans back from the crest, but the French were eventually obliged to give way, chiefly owing to artillery fire. Maire's Brigade, moving north of Elsasshausen, counter-attacked towards Woerth, reaching the village, but they were driven back with heavy losses and withdrew towards Froeschweiler. Two battalions of the 36th Regiment counter-attacked towards Woerth from the direction of the Froeschweiler wood, but they also were driven back and retired into the wood. After the repulse of these counter-attacks, the Vth Corps was again able to advance, and at last hands were joined with the XIth Corps.

Things having been quiet on the French left for some time MacMahon had called upon Ducrot to send him what infantry he could spare to Elsasshausen. Ducrot sent two battalions, 96th Regiment, and 1½ battalions, 18th Regiment. Of these, 1 battalion, 96th Regiment, entered the Elsasshausen copse at about 3 p.m., and opened a heavy fire on the troops of the XIth Corps that were still lining the northern edge of the Niederwald. Half the battalion then charged and drove the Germans back into the wood, but the attack was not made in sufficient strength to gain any but a temporary success, and when the French gave way the Germans followed them up, and thus gained the Elsasshausen copse.

About the same time General Wolff led the 18th Regiment in a counter-attack from Froeschweiler towards Woerth, but met with only temporary success.

Meanwhile, Von Bose had ordered the artillery of the XIth Corps to move forward to the Galgenberg. Crossing the Sauer at Gunstett, and moving by the Hagenau high road, they now began to arrive, and coming into action on the Galgenberg, the guns were suitably placed to support an attack on Elsasshausen at ranges from 700 to 900 yards. The guns arrived most opportunely, as another counter-attack had all but started a panic in the infantry of the XIth Corps when the French were checked by the fire of the leading batteries and their escort. Supported by the fire of their artillery, the XIth Corps pressed on and captured Elsasshausen. The defence was supported to the last moment by 2 batteries which did not attempt to limber up till the German infantry were within 50 yards of them. They left 5 guns in the hands of the enemy.

The artillery of the Vth Corps was also ordered forward. Some of the batteries went towards Goersdorf to try and help the Ist Bavarians, but there was little opportunity for artillery support in this part of the field. The remainder endeavoured to get through Woerth, but they were much delayed by the confusion in the streets and did not reach the heights on the right bank of the Sauer till some time after the artillery of the XIth Corps had arrived on the Galgenberg.

The decisive attack

The crisis of the battle had now been reached. The French had been driven into a very narrow compass, and, as the German hold on Elsasshausen seemed secure, MacMahon decided to use his reserves to cover his retreat. At the same time, the German Official history says of the Germans that "the confusion and mixing up of units was so great, and the troops so exhausted, that to persevere to the end demanded all the confidence of Von Kirchbach, all the energy of the Chiefs, and the most absolute devotion of the troops."

From this time onwards the German higher commanders lost control of the battle, and could do little more than influence the troops in their immediate neighbourhood. The guns of the Vth and XIth Corps came up to within 900 yards of Froeschweiler, and all pressed on to the attack of the village which was the key of the position.

MacMahon still had at his disposal the following troops:

Pellé's Division (which had fought at Weissenburg), 2 battalions 50th Regiment, 2 battalions 74th Regiment, 3 battalions 1st Turcos.
Septeuil's Cavalry Brigade.
Bonnemain's Cavalry Division.
Reserve Artillery, 8 batteries.

The 50th and 74th Regiments formed the garrison of Froeschweiler which had been placed in a state of defence.

As the direction of the advance of the enemy from Elsasshausen was directly threatening his line of retreat from Froeschweiler on Reichshoffen, MacMahon decided to use his reserve troops to assist the withdrawal of the infantry by pressing back the enemy advancing from the south. First he ordered Bonnemain's cavalry to charge the enemy in the direction of Elsasshausen. The ground was unsuitable for cavalry action, though not to the same extent as that over which Michel's brigade had charged earlier in the day. There could, however, be no cohesion in the charge for this reason. Bodies of cavalry charged hither and thither east and west of Elsasshausen, and sacrificed themselves nobly. They gained a little time for the infantry, but accomplished nothing more.

Then the reserve artillery made an attempt to cover the retreat. The 8 batteries came into action on the rising ground just north-west of Elsasshausen, 4 batteries facing east, 2 facing south-east, and 2 facing south. The leading lines of the enemy's infantry were within 100 yards of them when they came into action. They opened fire rapidly and caused the enemy considerable losses, but at once men and horses were shot down, and the situation could not possibly last. The order was given for the guns to be withdrawn, and no less than 31 guns were safely limbered up and taken out of action, 17 being left in the hands of the enemy.

The acts of heroism of individual drivers, who with a limber and a pair of horses succeeded, with the assistance of the gunners, in limbering up the guns one by one and withdrawing them, call to mind those of the drivers of Q Battery, Royal Horse Artillery, at Sauna's Post. But we must remember that the one took place at a distance of 100 yards from a mass of victorious infantry, while the other was at a range of not much less than 1,000 yards. Such is the change in the effect of fire in 30 years.

After the withdrawal of the guns, MacMahon called upon the 1st Turcos for a final effort. This gallant regiment, which had fought so bravely and lost so heavily at Weissenburg, responded nobly to his appeal. They deployed behind the crest where the guns came into action, advanced and fired a volley, but retired a little disordered. Then re-arranging the ranks, they advanced again and charged through the leading ranks of the Germans, through Elsasshausen driving the enemy out of the houses, through the copse, and three times attempted to reach the northern edge of the Niederwald. But here they were brought up by fresh troops and were heavily fired on from both flanks. They were literally shot to pieces, and, retiring through the copse, reached the edge of the Grosswald, where they remained till their ammunition was exhausted, when they withdrew through the wood.

While these events were taking place, a brigade of the Wurtemburg Division of Von Werder's Corps crossed the Sauer at Gunstett with orders from the Crown Prince to move on Reichshoffen. Hearing, however, from Prussian officers that the XIth Corps was hard pressed about Elsasshausen, the Commander diverted his march in that direction, and arrived in time to take part in the attack on Froeschweiler.

The attack on the French left made little progress. The 2nd Turcos offered a heroic resistance to the 1st Bavarians in the Froeschweiler wood, assisted by the 1st Zouaves. The fight was continued in the wood till 4.45 p.m., by which time the Turcos had practically ceased to exist, their losses during the day's fighting, including prisoners, amounting to the enormous figure of 92 per cent of their officers, and 85 per cent of their men.

The 3rd Division, IInd Bavarians, did not reach Langensultzbach till 3 p.m., and was not seriously engaged. Ducrot however ordered the retreat of his division owing to the collapse of the French right, and formed a rearguard on the edge of the Grosswald.

The attack on Froeschweiler was supported by 84 guns at very close range, but the village was not captured till 5 p.m. MacMahon stayed in the village till just before its capture, gave orders for the rearguard, saw it in position, and then rode to Reichshoffen, where he telegraphed to the Emperor and gave orders for his troops to make for Saverne. The French retreated in great disorder, some going to Bitche, some to Saverne, and some to Strasburg.

Lespart's Division of the Vth Corps reached Niederbronn at 4 p.m., having marched very slowly on account of the heat.

The German 4th Cavalry Division did not leave its bivouac at Shoenenburg, and was not available for pursuit. Five detachments were formed by different Corps consisting of Divisional Cavalry, Artillery, and, in some cases, Infantry. They were directed on Gundershoffen, Reichshoffen, and Neiderbronn. Some insignificant captures were effected, but in no case was the pursuit carried more than five miles. Touch was lost with the enemy and the troops returned.

The losses were French, 20,000; German, 11,000.

Chapter VI

Comments on the Battle of Woerth

It is now proposed to comment on certain incidents and aspects of the battle in order primarily to bring out those lessons which are applicable to the present day, and to apply the teaching .of our Field Service Regulations and Training Manuals to those questions which must necessarily be influenced by present-day conditions.

The occupation of the position

Before considering the defects in MacMahon's dispositions, and how the distribution of the available troops might have been improved, it is necessary to draw attention once again to the ground. From Neehweiler to the Hagenau Forest, measured in a line along the crest of the Froeschweiler ridge, is a distance of some six miles, and in the space which is included between the crest of the ridge and the Sauer there are two open areas and two wooded areas. Of these, the wooded areas could be defended with comparative ease as the event showed the open area between Froeschweiler and Elsasshausen was strong against a frontal attack, and lent itself to a defence in depth, but was unsuitable for the action of cavalry; while the area between the Niederwald and the Hagenau Forest was suitable for the action of the three arms in combination, and was, therefore, clearly indicated as that in which to prepare for counter-attack. This circumstance, moreover, fitted well with the strategical aspect of the defence of the position, for, as has already been pointed out, the French right flank was strategically vulnerable.

MacMahon's dispositions have been subjected to the following criticisms:

1. They were too linear and lacked depth.
2. The troops occupied the position prematurely and before the direction of the enemy's attack could be foreseen.
3. His cavalry and reserves were unsuitably placed.
4. He had taken few if any steps to strengthen the position, and failed to utilize the strong points of the position to economize men and so increase the strength of his reserves.

Let us consider these points:

1. Our Field Service Regulations say that "the defence must have freedom of manœuvre, which demands sufficient depth ..." On the subject of the organization of a battlefield for defence they say further that "though the extent of ground actually held, when the direction of the enemy's advance is definitely known, must be strictly limited by the numbers available, the extent of ground reconnoitred and prepared for occupation may be larger, and should admit of various alternative distributions of the force to meet various courses of action open to the enemy."

As the Chief of the Imperial General Staff has pointed out, in a recent Memorandum on Army Training, that at our field exercises dispositions for defence are often too linear,[1]

1. See also an article by Lieut.-Colonel Schreiber, R.E., in *The Army Review* for January, 1912, p. 121, entitled "Defensive Tactics," and a lecture by Major G. D. Swinton, R.E., in the *R.A. Journal* for February, 1912,

General Bonnal's views on the organization of the Woerth position, in depth are especially interesting. He advocates the organization of the defence in three lines:–

(i) Langensultzbach – eastern edge of Froeschweiler wood – Hagenau high road Woerth – Hagenau high road – Eastern edge of Niederwald – thence towards Durrenbach.

(ii) Neehweiler-Froeschweiler-Elsasshausen-Albrechtshauserhof – with Morsbronn and Forstheim held as posts in advance of the right flank.

(iii) Niederbronn-Reichshoffen-Gundershoffen.

It will be noticed that these dispositions, though primarily designed to meet an attack from the east, are capable of modification to meet an attack from the south-east, or south, the most likely alternatives. This exactly accords with the principle, laid down in the extract from the Field Service Regulations quoted above.

The suggested dispositions raise the important question of the use of advanced posts. Our Regulations place limitations on their use, stating that they are a "weakness if exposed to artillery fire which cannot be answered, and if they cannot be supported by effective infantry fire." If, on the other hand, they can be so supported, they are said to be "of value in breaking up an attack."

Bonnal's first line hardly corresponds with this conception, it being difficult to co-operate with the defence of Langensultzbach or Morsbronn from the main position, though the defence of Woerth could be assisted by artillery fire from the Froeschweiler ridge. But possibly the views of the General Staff are undergoing some modification on this subject, as the memorandum on Army Training above referred to advocates the use of advanced posts and advanced troops for the purposes of gaining time, of breaking up the enemy's attack, and of using up his troops.

The degree of resistance that is offered by such posts must, however, be carefully regulated in accordance with the functions they are called upon to perform. Unless the situation imperatively demands their sacrifice for some definite reason such as to allow deployment to take place or the arrival of reinforcements, their resistance should not be unduly prolonged unless they can be supported by fire from the main position, and their action should conform to that laid down for a force engaged in delaying action.

Bonnal's choice of the line of the Hagenau high road in preference to the crests of the spurs between the Froeschweiler wood and the Niederwald is interesting. The field of fire, the facilities for withdrawing and exposure to the enemy's fire, are the factors in the case, and they are nicely balanced. At first sight it would appear that it would be easier to withdraw from the crests of the spurs, but Bonnal considers that the cover in the re-entrants makes them good lines of retreat, and that the passages of the river can be kept under a more effective rifle fire from the line of the road. If the line of the road is selected, however, the Galgenberg is too important a tactical feature to be left undefended.

As regards the 2nd or main line of defence, Infantry Training, 1911, Sec. 143, emphasizes the importance of occupying and strengthening localities of special tactical importance, so that they may form pivots on which to hinge the defence of the remainder of the position. The defences of these localities should be arranged so that they may give each other mutual support, and the intervening ground should be used for local counterattacks. The tactical points in this position are Neehweiler, the high ground at the head of the clearing, Froeschweiler, the knoll between Froeschweiler and Elsasshausen, Elsasshausen, the Elsasshausen copse, the Alberchtshausserhof, point 222. The majority

entitled "The Tactical Employment of Field Defences."

of these are self-supporting, but some are not. For instance, the Niederwald protrudes between the Elsasshausen copse and the Albrechtshauserhof.

It will be noticed that several villages are included amongst these important tactical points, which raises the question of the suitability of villages for defence in view of the effect of modern artillery fire. In this case the villages would not be subject to accurate artillery fire till the guns had crossed the Sauer and taken up positions on the right bank, no easy matter under modern conditions.

The prevention of penetration between the tactical points, especially when they are not self-supporting, must be provided for either by holding the intervals or by posting suitable local reserves for counter-attack in rear of them.

Bonnal's third line in the valley of the Falkensteinerbach is a measure of precaution similar in its effect to the occupation and strengthening of supporting points in rear of an attack.

2. MacMahon's troops bivouacked on the night of the 5th August on the positions in which they fought, and thus sacrificed their power of manœuvre to a considerable extent. On this point the Field Service Regulations say: "The Cavalry must discover the direction of march and the strength of the hostile columns, and until the former is known the force should not be deployed, even when the enemy's line of advance may be foreseen. A force which is kept in hand covered by the necessary protective troops is able to assume the offensive at once if a turn in the tide of events makes this advisable." A force which is kept in hand can also meet an attack from an unforeseen direction, or retire with greater ease than one which is deployed, considerations of some importance to MacMahon. A more suitable disposition on the evening of the 5th than that adopted would have been as follows: – The 1st, 3rd, and 4th Divisious under cover of the Froeschweiler ridge in the neighbourhood of Neehweiler, Froeschweiler, and Eberbach respectively, with outposts on the Sauer from Langensultzbach to Morsbronn, and the 2nd Division, Du Mesnil's Division, such of the Cavalry as were not in touch with the enemy, and Reserve Artillery in the valley of the Falkensteinerbach, about Reichshoffen and Gundershoffen.

3. The necessity to protect the right flank has already been pointed out. If the reserves, instead of being placed immediately in the rear of the centre about Froeschweiler, had been placed as suggested about Reichshoffen and Gundershoffen they could have taken position in the morning under cover of the Forstheim ridge, where they would have had full liberty of manœuvre, and while remaining concealed, could have chosen their own time and direction for counter-attack.

4. MacMahon had done little if any entrenching, and had not even destroyed the bridges over the Sauer. Ducrot appears to have made urgent representations to him on the 5th in favour of strengthening the villages and other tactical points on the position. MacMahon, supported by all the other subordinate commanders, refused to fatigue the troops; surely a mistaken policy unless he had decided to retire, which was not the case.

The Field Service Regulations say: "The amount of preparation possible depends on the time available, which in turn depends on the strategical situation," and for this reason Infantry Training says that the preparation of the position for defence may have to be undertaken at the last moment, and must be of a hasty nature." But French troops had been on the Woerth position for sufficient time to have strengthened it considerably, and a battle on the position was at any rate contemplated. The fear of fatiguing the troops, therefore, can hardly be accepted as an adequate reason for not entrenching.

The natural strength of the left of the position was not recognized by MacMahon as he allotted the defence of this flank to Ducrot's Division, the strongest numerically in the army.

Reconnaissance when troops are in touch

Von Walther's reconnaissance has been universally condemned, and the use of artillery in such circumstances has been held to have been inexcusable. Lartigue's reconnaissance was equally blameworthy, and might well have precipitated the battle, if Von Walther's had not already done so. The Field Service Regulations say that when outposts are in touch reconnaissance is limited to patrols. "Reconnoitring patrols are sent out from the outposts with the object of watching the enemy if the opposing forces are in close touch." And again "Detachments in close proximity to the enemy must be careful to avoid useless collisions."

The moral of Woerth, however, is that when troops are in close touch a Commander cannot always choose his own time for action, and that his staff must be more than usually careful to keep all subordinate commanders informed of his intentions.

Action of advanced guards

The action of the German advanced guards was disconnected, as was inevitable in the circumstances, and resulted in the repulse with heavy losses of a considerable proportion of three Army Corps, amounting to 17,000 men. In considering the action of the German advanced guards it is necessary to remember that Woerth was not a battle of encounter, but was brought on by the ill-considered action of a subordinate commander against the wishes of the Chief Command. The excuse has been put forward for the German Commanders that, trained as they were themselves to the use of advanced guards and advanced troops, it was reasonable for them to expect that their advanced guards would first encounter advanced troops of the enemy, which it would be necessary for them to drive in before the enemy's position could be reconnoitred and a plan of attack formed. Had the army been on the march without the knowledge that a considerable French force was occupying the Woerth position, such a plea might be accepted. But we know that the Crown Prince expected MacMahon to concentrate his available forces and give battle on this position. Every German Corps Commander must have known, if he had given the matter a moment's thought, that any troops launched across the Sauer must very shortly become engaged with considerable forces of the enemy.

Moreover, if we consider the manner in which these advanced guards became engaged, the excuse is obviously an afterthought.

The 4th Bavarian Division advanced to attack the French left flank under the misapprehension that the French were attacking the Vth Corps. In anticipation of such a contingency arising both brigades composing the division had deployed before touch was gained with the enemy. When the sound of the guns was heard the division advanced thus on a broad front, and by no stretch of the imagination can the dispositions made be said to conform with the idea of using an advanced guard to drive in the enemy's advanced troops preparatory to a main attack.

The advanced guard of the XIth Corps was drawn into the fight by Lartigue's attempt to capture the Bruchmill. The troops composing it attacked the enemy and crossed the Sauer on their own initiative, which was not only contrary to the spirit of the orders issued by the Crown Prince, but contrary to the intention of the Divisional Commander, who wished to establish a defensive position on the left bank of the Sauer.

The 20th Brigade, Vth Corps, was on outpost, and was not an advanced guard in the ordinary sense of the term. The reasons that led Von Kirchbach to order such a small force to "occupy Woerth and the heights beyond" are somewhat obscure, as has already been explained, but it is quite possible that his motive was to gain a footing on the right bank of the river in order to facilitate the crossing of the main body of his Corps. If such was the case the task was appropriate for an advanced guard, and Von Kirchbach can only be blamed for employing insufficient force for the purpose.

We see then that the German attacks during the early stages of the battle have little in common with the normal action of advanced guards in a battle of encounter, and that they failed because they were disconnected and made with insufficient forces. They were disconnected because the battle was entered upon against the wishes of the German Commander, who was, therefore, unable to co-ordinate the different efforts. The forces proved to be insufficient for the purposes of a preparatory action, because the French advanced line was separated by a very short space from the main position, and the second line troops were freely used to maintain the integrity of the advanced line. When all this is granted, however, it must be admitted that these attacks did much towards reconnoitring the enemy's dispositions and fixing him in his position, both of which are important functions of the troops assigned to the preparatory action.

The lesson for us appears to be that, if advanced guards are to be successful in driving in the enemy's advanced troops and reconnoitring his position, the intention of the Commander to attack must be clear, the co-operation of the different advanced guards advancing by different roads must be assured by lateral communication, and troops must be at hand to support those that are first engaged. If these conditions are absent, a succession of repulses is to be expected.

Conduct of the Battle by the Crown Prince

The Crown Prince was responsible for two errors in connexion with the battle which might have had far-reaching effect. The first, in not communicating to the Commander of the Vth Corps the instructions which he issued on the 5th August to the Commander of the IInd Bavarians. This was a failure in the performance of Staff duties its effect has been pointed out, and the point need not be laboured. The second was his order issued at 10 a.m. to Von Kirchbach "not to continue the struggle and to avoid everything that may induce a fresh one." This order, based as it was on imperfect information, placed the Commander of the Vth Corps in an embarrassing position to which further reference will be made later.

Although the sound of heavy firing was heard at Soultz at 9 a.m., it was not till 11 a.m. that the Crown Prince was persuaded by his Chief of the Staff, Von Blumenthal, to move with all haste to the scene of action. Field telegraphs and telephones and the signal service generally have been so developed of recent years that the idea prevails that the Headquarters of an Army will, in the future, be far removed from the field of battle. If we are to judge from the experiences of Manchuria, and the common practice at manœuvres, there is more than a little justification for this view. At the same time, a word of caution, based on what occurred at Woerth, is necessary. The report of the Officer of the Headquarter Staff sent forward by the Crown Prince left the field at 9.30

a.m. The Crown Prince received it at Soultz in half-an-hour, and half-an-hour later an order based upon it was received by Von Kirchbach. Not bad going it must be admitted, and considering the congestion which often arises in field telegraph offices on important occasions, it is doubtful whether more rapid transmission can be assured. And yet events had moved too fast to justify the Crown Prince in acting on information half-an-hour old.

If we look at the ground we find that an admirable comprehensive view of the battlefield can be obtained from the Dieffenbach ridge, and the Crown Prince would probably have been well-advised to have taken up his position there at least two hours earlier than he did. In these days the same argument applies. No doubt the position selected would be further withdrawn than that actually taken up by the Crown Prince, on account of the increased range of Artillery, and if the telegraphic headquarters were to remain at Soultz as a matter of convenience, a wire would be run forward to the position actually selected. It cannot be admitted that the signal service absolves a commander from responsibility for personal reconnaissance.

The hurried arrival of the Headquarters on the field of battle does not appear to have contributed to clear thinking. There was evidently much anxiety and want of knowledge as to the situation for some little time after the Crown Prince arrived, which is but natural in the circumstances. The situation, however, gradually unfolded itself as reports were received, and it then became possible for the Commander of the army to intervene with effect. The first impulse had been to order all available troops to come to the assistance of the Vth Corps, but calmer counsels soon prevailed.

The orders that were issued by the Crown Prince at 1.30 p.m. give a fair indication of the views that prevailed in the German army at the time as to the conduct of an action. It will be remembered that the Vth Corps was ordered to defer its attacks till those on the flanks could take effect; the XIth Corps was directed to continue its turning movement and make Froeschweiler its objective while the extreme flanks, the IInd Bavarians and the Wurtemberg Division, were directed on a point well in rear of the French position, namely Reichshoffen. That neither the IInd Bavarians nor the Wurternburg Division ever reached Reichshoffen was only a failure in execution. The idea underlying the order was evidently envelopment of both the enemy's flanks, and the delaying of the attack of the Vth Corps seems to contain the germ of the theory of simultaneous pressure. The troops held in hand were one division of the Ist Bavarians, the 4th Cavalry Division, and the Baden Division, the last-named being specially told off to protect the left flank. There is nothing here indicative of the preparatory action along the whole battle front, to be followed by the decisive attack at a selected point, which is the underlying principle of our Field Service Regulations.

It is interesting to note how the envelopment theory miscarried on this occasion. The IInd Bavarians were in no condition to attack, and a Brigade of the Wurtemburg Division, after crossing the Sauer at Gunstett, is said to have been diverted from its objective by appeals for assistance from the XIth Corps, and moved on Froeschweiler. Not a man moved in the direction of Reichshoffen.

The Crown Prince must be held responsible for the failure to make use of the Cavalry during the battle, and for the total absence of energetic pursuit. Cavalry, as the reserve of the army in an offensive action, is foreign to all our ideas on the subject. The outer flank of the XIth Corps in the Rhine plain was the obvious position for the 4th Cavalry Division and further reference will be made to this subject.

The conduct of the battle by Marshal MacMahon

Several points in MacMahon's generalship have already been referred to. His failure to concentrate his available forces, his decision to fight on the Woerth position, the distribution of his troops, his failure to provide for the protection of his right flank, and the position of his reserves. There remain some few points still to be discussed.

The position occupied by MacMahon during the battle was under a walnut tree near the road leading from Elsasshausen to Woerth. The view of the battlefield from this position differs materially from that which could be obtained from the position taken up by the Crown Prince on the opposite bank of the Sauer. The one is as circumscribed as the other is comprehensive. The Niederwald and the Froeschweiler wood blot out all view of the flanks. No doubt MacMahon's absorption in the task of repelling the attacks of the Vth Corps was largely due to this fact. He would probably have obtained a more comprehensive grasp of the events that were taking place if he had selected a position a little further removed from the scene of the actual fighting on the crest of the ridge between Froeschweiler and Elsasshausen.

If MacMahon was wrong to accept battle at Woerth, should he have broken off the engagement if a favourable opportunity occurred? It is easy to be wise after the event, and no doubt either at 11.30 a.m., or at 2.30 p.m., he could have broken off the fight and withdrawn his army with considerable credit to himself and his troops. They had inflicted heavy losses on the Germans, and inspired them in all probability with a wholesome respect for their fighting capacity. Ducrot's Division had not been seriously engaged and could have covered the retreat of the army.

On this question the French Official History quotes a passage from Montholon's *Memoirs of Napoleon* dealing with a similar incident, which is so appropriate that it will bear repeating:

> Des observateurs d'un esprit ordinaire diront qu'il eût dû se servir de l'aile qui était encore intacte pour opérer sa retraite et ne pas hasarder son reste. Mais avec de tels principes, un général est certain de manquer touter les occasions de succès et d'être constamment battu. La gloire et l'honneur des armes est le premier devoir qu'un général qui livre bataille doit considérer. Le salut and la conservation des hommes n'est que secondaire, mais c'est aussi dans cette audace et dans cette opinâtreté que se trouve le salut and la conservation des hommes. La conduite de Condé est done à imiter. Elle conforme a l'esprit, aux règles et aux cœurs des guerriers. S'il eut tort de livrer bataille dans la position qu'occupait. Merçy, il fit bien de ne jamais dêsespérer tant qu'il lui restait des braves aux drapeaux.

That is the spirit which animated MacMahon, to whom all honour is due for his determination.

We must admit, however, that he failed to coordinate the offensive efforts of his troops. Admirable as were many of the counter-attacks as regards the method of their execution, it is certain that his resources were thereby frittered away. The counter-attacks were all local in character, they were mostly directed against the frontal attack of the Vth Corps, which was the least promising direction, and no concerted effort was made against the flank of the XIthCorps, although there can be little question that suitable opportunities were offered. An attack directed against the flank of the Morsbronn column before it entered the Niederwald might have paralysed the turning movement, and an attack against the flank of the XIth Corps when it emerged from the Niederwald, might have had far-reaching results. But the assembly of a strong general reserve for a great counterstroke was no part of MacMahon's plan, and he appears to have aimed solely at repelling the onslaught made on his position.

Lastly, there is the question of the employment of his cavalry. They were unsuitably placed, used on unsuitable ground, and their action was confined to self-sacrificing efforts to cover the infantry retreat. To this subject we will return.

The Front on which the battle was fought

The subjects dealt with up to now all involve questions of principle in the consideration of which the value of the lessons of the past can hardly be gainsaid. The front on which a force of a given size can fight under modern conditions is a subject on which there is room for speculation and difference of opinion. At Woerth the French fought with 46,000 men on a front of somewhat less than four miles. Or, in other words, 11,500 men to a mile, or between 6 and 7 men to a yard. Yet they certainly had not too many men for the position, in fact, their reserves were weak.

The Vth Corps attacked on a front of 2,200 yards, or 10 men to a yard, and they were used up to the last man. The XIth Corps attacked on a front of 7 men to a yard, and by the time they reached the northern edge of the Niederwald, there were only 3 battalions left in reserve.

The lesson of Woerth is the necessity for depth in the distribution of the troops for battle, both in attack and defence, and it would be most unwise to ignore it. Yet a very marked tendency to over-extend the front has been noticeable in our manœuvre training, and has elicited unfavourable comment from the Chief of the Imperial General Staff.[2]

This over-extension of the front has perhaps been due to a variety of causes. Firstly, in some cases a confusion has existed between the undoubted necessity for infantry to extend when advancing under fire, and the extension of the front on which a force of a given size can fight. The former has been conclusively proved by all recent experience, but it is no excuse for the adoption of exaggerated ideas with respect to the latter.

Then there was a misreading of the most recent lessons of South Africa and Manchuria.

The front was unduly extended in South Africa on account of the exceptional conditions. The Boers were all mounted. When attacked and threatened with envelopment by superior numbers, they used their mobility to prolong the line and prevent envelopment. They were content to maintain their position, and seldom or never aimed at decisive results by means of counterattack. Their mobility enabled them to escape the natural consequences of such tactics, which would have overtaken a force composed principally of infantry.

Manchuria was conspicuous for bad communications, which enabled the lines of operation to be foreseen some time beforehand. The Russians, who usually fought on the defensive, were thus able to employ field fortification to a very large extent. Men were economized, and the front considerably extended, without risking penetration unduly.

Lastly, there is the effect of manoeuvre training in peace time. The necessity for depth is not apparent at manoeuvres. The front line seldom gives way, and if it does so by order of an Umpire, its recuperative powers are usually remarkable. There is an absence of disorder amongst defeated troops, and there is no loss of moral. On the other hand, the

2. Memorandum on Army Training, 1909, page 5; also 1910, page 5.

effect of envelopment is at once apparent. Possibly, for these reasons, there is a decided temptation to over-extend and dispense with reserves at manœuvres.

The Field Service Regulations, however, give us a valuable guide, and lay down that "a smaller force than 3 to 5 men per yard on the front on which the decisive attack is to be delivered will rarely prove sufficient, this force being distributed in such depth as circumstances make advisable."[3]

The increased power of the modern rifle has been used as an argument for a great reduction of the number of men employed on a given front, provided that a sufficient volume of fire is developed. But we have not yet reached a point at which we rely on fire alone, and the basis of our conception of the modern fight is the attainment of fire superiority as the necessary preliminary to the assault with the bayonet. As long as this conception holds the field, the value of numbers at the decisive point cannot be ignored.

The assumption of responsibility by the German Commanders and their loyal co-operation

Although the German commanders were not provided with a system of communication such as we have at the present day, they frequently communicated with one another, as well as with Headquarters, and they were imbued with the doctrine of full assumption of responsibility and loyal cooperation one with another. The result was that, although there was every excuse for hesitation and inaction during the early hours of the battle, the evil results of the irregular manner in which the action started were reduced to a minimum.

The Commander of the Vth Corps renewed the attack on his own responsibility. The flanks then broke off the engagement in accordance with orders from the Crown Prince, but when called upon by the Commander of the Vth Corps to renew the action, the Commander of the XIth Corps agreed to do so as soon as he was fully informed of the state of affairs.

Von Kirchbach put aside the order of the Crown Prince to break off the fight. But the circumstances demanded the exercise of his own judgment. The guiding rule of conduct in such cases is stated in Field Service Regulations, Section 12, to be: "A departure from either the spirit or the letter of an order is justified if the subordinate who assumes the responsibility bases his decision on some fact which could not be known to the officer who issued the order, and if he is conscientiously satisfied that he is acting as his superior, if present, would order him to act."

Henderson quotes the ruling of the Duke of Wellington in a similar case: – "Major-General Wellesley thinks it proper to explain to the troops that there is much difference in the situation and cases in which an officer is permitted to exercise his discretion. It very frequently happens that an order may be given to an officer, which, from circumstances not known to the person who gave it at the time he gave it, would be impossible to execute, or the difficulty or risk of the execution of it would be so great as to amount to a moral impossibility. In a case of this kind Major-General Wellesley is by no means disposed to check officers detached in the exercise of their discretion; but Capt. —'s case is not of this description; he could have had no information which the officer had not who gave him his orders, and it was his duty to obey." Here, then, we have a principle which has survived a century of war without any modification whatever.

3. Field Service Regulations, Section 104. See also an article communicated to the *Army Review*, April 1912, "Frontage; Extension and Depth of formations in Attack and Defence."

While, however, Von Bose's action in engaging the full strength of his corps at the request of Von Kirchbach is highly to be commended, and the assumption of responsibility by Von Kirchbach in ignoring the orders of the Crown Prince was fully justified, there were several instances during the day of the abuse of initiative.

The action of Von Walther and Lartigue in conducting reconnaissances in the early morning has already been discussed and condemned.

The passage of the Sauer and the attack of the Niederwald by the advanced guard of the XIth Corps was undertaken on the initiative of the officers with the troops, was contrary to the intention of their commander, and, though excused by the German Official History on the grounds that the troops could not remain where they were, and that it was better to go forward than back, was hardly justified by the circumstances.

Von Schkopp's action in diverting his brigade from the line of march assigned to it, and sending only a portion of his command to Gunstett when ordered to form the reserve, while he persevered with the remainder and such troops as he could collect, is also excused by the German Official History on the grounds that Von Schkopp could not send back the 94th Regiment, which was engaged with the enemy near Durrenbach. This is a fiction, as the regiment was not engaged at the time, and Von Schkopp was guilty of an act of indiscipline, which should not be condoned simply because it had very happy results.

Finally, the Commander of the Wurtemburg Brigade received orders from the Crown Prince to move on Reichshoffen after passing the Sauer at Gunstett, obviously with the intention of completing the envelopment of the French right flank and operating against their line of retreat. We have seen how again the German Official History endeavours to excuse this officer for going to Froeschweiler by saying that he was appealed to by Prussian officers to go to the assistance of the XIth Corps. Such an excuse would not hold by the light of our Field Service Regulations, or the ruling of the Duke of Wellington. The Crown Prince must have known that the XIth Corps must inevitably become hotly engaged near Elsasshausen when he issued his order to the Wurtemburg Brigade, and it was the duty of the officer in command to comply.

We see, therefore, both the good and the evil effects of the training of officers to assume responsibility. It is not every officer's judgment that can be trusted. But the lesson of Woerth undoubtedly is that the good greatly outweighs the evil.

The combination of holding attacks and turning movements

The term "holding attack" has been expunged from our Training Manuals as liable to be misinterpreted. Troops ordered to attack are invariably to attack with the utmost vigour, as it is recognized that no mere demonstration will hold the enemy to his ground and use up his reserves so that the decisive attack may have full effect. In Field Service Regulations, Section 103, it is said "the term decisive attack does not imply that the influence of other attacks is indecisive, but rather that it is the culmination of gradually increasing pressure relentlessly applied to the enemy at all points from the moment when contact with him is first obtained." And again, "the general principle is that the enemy must be engaged in sufficient strength to pin him to his ground and to wear down his power of resistance, while the force allotted to the decisive attack must be as strong as possible."

These principles, so far as they apply to the conduct of a holding attack, are admirably illustrated by the battle of Woerth. The attacks of the Vth Corps were made with the utmost vigour, and they used up the French reserves continuously throughout. the day.

Every fresh attack drew in fresh troops to counter-attack, till ultimately Von Kirchbach, with the approval of the Crown Prince, did not hesitate to put in his last battalion. The vigour of these attacks monopolized MacMahon's attention and diverted his mind from the importance of the turning movement of the XIth Corps. If the Vth Corps had contented itself with a mere frontal demonstration, can it be supposed that MacMahon would not have concentrated his reserves against the XIth Corps, and who can say what might have been the result of the battle if he had done so?

Again, the attack of the XIth Corps against the Morsbronn ridge illustrates the same principle. The columns that crossed the Sauer at Spachbach and Gunstett, and attacked the Niederwald and the Albrecthshauserhof, fully occupied the attention of Lartigue. These attacks were pressed with determination; they were supported by a great mass of artillery and they drew in and used up the French reserves. When the turning movement through Morsbronn developed, there were few troops left to meet it, and the full effect of an enveloping attack was felt at once. As we have seen, the position could not be maintained without a counter offensive, for which inadequate troops were available.

Here then is a lesson of abiding value, but it is not possible to leave this subject without referring again to a point which has already been discussed. The extracts quoted above from the Field Service Regulations foreshadow a decisive attack as a separate act. It is true that in one passage it is described as the "culmination of a gradually increasing pressure," but in the preceding sentence it is said that "a force must be held in readiness to deliver the decisive attack, while the remainder is employed to develop the attack, and to wear down the enemy's power of resistance." Woerth was not fought on this principle. In the description of the battle the final attack on Froeschweiler has been termed the "decisive attack." The only fresh body of troops that took part in this attack was the Wurtemburg Brigade, which had certainly not been kept in hand for the purpose. If the Crown Prince's orders had been complied with the attack on Froeschweiler would have been carried out solely by the already exhausted infantry of the Vth and XIth Corps, and the principal object of these orders, as has already been explained, appears to have been to ensure simultaneous pressure by strong bodies of troops enveloping both flanks.

The above must not be taken as an adverse criticism of our Regulations, but merely as an example of a difference in doctrine.

Breaking up formations in the deployment and the mixing of units in the final stages

One of the principal features of the battle was the confusion which arose in the ranks of the attacking infantry during the later phases. This is attributed by most writers on the subject to the breaking up of the organization of the Divisions, Brigades, and Regiments in the initial deployment. This was again due to the haste with which the troops were thrown into the fight. The principal example was in the XIth Corps. The manner in which both the advanced guard and the main body of the corps were brought into action has been fully explained in the description of the battle, and it is not necessary to repeat the details. It will suffice to point out that the confusion, which eventually arose, might possibly have been less if the initial deployment had taken place with less haste and more regard for the preservation of the control of the subordinate commanders.

The French Official History considers that the mixing of units in the final stages was largely attributable to the undue initiative allowed to the company and section officers during peace training. Each was eager for distinction, and made full use of the initiative allowed to him to press forward in any direction that seemed to him best at the moment. Portions of the same company thus frequently diverged from the original objective. If this is a legitimate criticism, then this mixing of units is likely to be aggravated rather than reduced in the battles of the future, for it is certain that modern conditions demand increased exercise of initiative, not only from officers, but from individual soldiers. At any rate the lesson of Woerth is that, while every step should be taken to minimize this evil, it is one that must be reckoned with, and that any tactical theories which ignore it are not likely to prove practical in war.[4] The only way to reduce the confusion that must inevitably arise is to insist, as does our Infantry Training, on the necessity for re-forming the ranks after the capture of every locality. Bonnal quotes three examples of this in the XIth Corps. The troops that captured the Albrechtshauserhof were in the act of reforming when they were counter-attacked by the mixed units of Lartigue's Division. They were again thrown into confusion. Von Schkopp's column was re-forming after passing through Morsbronn when the charge of the Cuirassier Brigade took place. Again, later, after moving up the Eberbach valley and passing the Western end of the Niederwald, the 94th Regiment of Von Schkopp's Brigade re-formed, and it was largely due to the renewed order in the ranks of this regiment that the counter-attack of the 1st Turcos was repulsed.

It is impossible to read the official histories without being struck by the fact that the German corps commanders frequently issued orders to brigades over the heads of the divisional commanders. In fact, as soon as the corps were committed to action, they seem to have fought by brigades and not by divisions. These remarks of course apply only to the Prussian corps, as the two Bavarian Corps only had one division of each corps engaged. But the fact remains that a corps of two divisions of two brigades each is not a very handy organization on the battlefield, and this organization is almost bound to tend to the suppression of the divisional commanders. These officers can have had no very clearly defined duties throughout the day in either the Vth or XIth Corps.

Conduct of the fire fight

Henderson considers that the weapons used in 1870 "at once brought into prominence the characteristic which makes all fighting from 1870 onwards so different from the fighting of any previous war. The attainment of superiority of fire became the decisive factor, and the assault with the bayonet lost the importance which had hitherto belonged to it." Our Regulations have for many years looked upon the attainment of superiority of fire as the necessary preliminary to a successful assault, but we still look to the assault as an essential element in the fight, and do not believe that a stubborn enemy can be shot out of his position. At the same time, the conduct of the fire fight has undergone considerable modification since 1870.

The Germans at Woerth deployed and moved forward with the leading line in "line of company columns at deploying interval." No extension took place till the effect of rifle fire made this necessary, when each company threw out a line of skirmishers of about one-third of its strength, the remainder advancing in column of sections.

The second line advanced as a rule in "line of company columns at deploying interval," but these columns usually deployed when they came under heavy fire.

4. This question is dealt with fully in "A Summer Night's Dream," translated from the German by Capt. Gawne and published in the *U.S. Magazine*, 1890.

In some cases there was a third line, while in others there was not.

Losses began to be felt at about 900 yards, but the attackers were usually able to advance to within 500 yards without halting or firing. They then occupied a fire position,[5] and entered on a struggle for fire supremacy. If they were successful in this, the further advance was not as a rule accompanied by much difficulty or loss. They were frequently counter-attacked and driven from their fire position, and were seldom successful in establishing fire superiority till they were closely supported by their artillery.

The Germans were trained to the use of volleys and "file firing" or independent fire, but it is clear that the officers very soon lost control, and that "file firing" was the rule and not the exception. The men also frequently fired on the move. The following extracts from Regimental Histories are quoted by Henderson: "The officers gave the signal to advance, and the whole line of skirmishers went up the hill with hurrahs, and a fabulously rapid fire." "I saw no enemy in our front, but we kept up uninterruptedly a very hot fire." "Then, however, the enemy's line all at once turned about and ran away; we followed, shouting hurrah, and firing all the time." It is clear from these extracts that there was much excitement and not much control of fire.

There is room for speculation as to the best manner in which to conduct an advance and attain the necessary fire superiority on the modern battlefield. Since the days of Woerth, although the theory of fire superiority remains the same, improvements in weapons have greatly modified methods, and it is in this domain essentially that it is necessary to keep abreast of improvements and to endeavour to forecast their effect.

To state our present-day theory in a few words – we admit no normal formation in attack, and insist on formations being suited to the ground – we recognize the necessity for extension when moving under fire, but we endeavour to remain in formed bodies as long as possible so as to facilitate control of movement – movement under fire is made by rushes, the number of men making a rush and the length of the rush being dependent on the volume and effect of the enemy's fire – we use fire primarily to support movement – our object is to build up a firing line in close proximity to the enemy so that we may be able to overcome his fire and ultimately be able to deliver a successful assault – in order to control the expenditure of ammunition and to make the fire as effective as possible and ensure a suitable distribution, we endeavour to maintain an effective control of fire throughout.

The application of this theory to different cases is capable of infinite variety. Let us endeavour to apply it to a single case, say the first attack of the 20th Brigade, Vth Corps, on the Galgenberg. We will assume that 2 columns of 2 battalions each are allotted to the attack, one moving through Woerth and the other through Spachbach, as was the case. An examination of Map VII and Panoramas shows that the western slopes of the Dieffenbach ridge are fully exposed to artillery fire from the Froeschweiler ridge, and that there is very little cover on these slopes:. It will be necessary, therefore, for the battalions moving on Woerth to deploy under cover of the ridge. Those moving on Spachbach have a covered approach for some distance through the Fuchshübel wood. We must now examine the ground with a view to the selection of possible fire positions. The first that presents itself on the Spachbach line of approach is the line of the Goersdorf-Spachbach road, which

5. There was an essential difference in the ways in which the French and Germans formed a firing line. The French skirmishers fell back and withdrew through gaps in the line which was formed behind them. The Germans moved up into line with their skirmishers, who were absorbed in the firing line.

is about 1,200 yards from the nearest point of the enemy's position on the Galgenberg – then comes the river bank – then the meadows must be crossed before the railway is reached then comes the Hagenau high road, which forms a peculiar elbow at this point shortly afterwards dead ground is reached at the foot of the hill. On the Woerth line of approach there is no fire position for infantry till the western outskirts of Woerth itself are reached, and after debouching from the village, the road to Elsasshausen immediately climbs the western slopes of the Galgenberg.

Before launching the attack there are various points for the commander to consider – the attacks will be separated and must be properly timed so that they are not beaten in detail – artillery support – the use of his machine guns. The Spachbach column has further to go and the more difficult ground to traverse in the later stages. This must be allowed for. Artillery support will be dealt with later. Some machine guns should be established as soon as possible on the line of the Goersdorf-Spachbach road, and if a suitable approach to a good position could be found, it might be desirable to mass the guns of the brigade there to begin with. The first advance would be made with the object of gaining access to Woerth and Spachbach, and establishing a suitable force, say ½ battalion from the Spachbach column, on the line of the Goersdorf-Spachbach road to cover the further advance with fire. This advance, being through a zone swept by the enemy's artillery fire, would be made as rapidly as possible, the formation being that considered least vulnerable to artillery fire. The Woerth column would push on through the village and establish a firing line on the western outskirts.

During the progress of the attack the fire of each column must be directed so as to assist the progress of the other. This requires careful prearrangement. The Woerth column could establish a strong firing line and some machine guns in the south-western outskirts of the village, and by concentrating fire on the south-eastern slopes of the Galgenberg, would be able materially to assist the advance of the Spachbach column. This column must cross the river under artillery and long range rifle fire. The operation will be difficult, and engineers must make the necessary bridges. As soon as they are completed, an effort must be made to cross the meadows as rapidly as possible till the line of the railway is reached. In order to carry out this operation with success, covering fire from guns, machine guns, and rifles is essential, including the support of the Woerth column already alluded to. Provision must be made to protect both flanks of the attack, the firing lines must be gradually reinforced, and a further advance begun, again supported by fire till a footing is gained on the slopes of the hill. Both columns would now concentrate their fire on the Galgenberg and commence short rushes over the open ground, which lies between the position and the Hagenau road, supported by overhead fire. The rushes would, wherever possible, be made to cover over dead ground. Artillery support is now a vital factor, for, if it is efficient, the defenders will have great difficulty in firing on the leading lines, and it may be possible to assemble gradually under the crest of the hill a sufficient force to deliver a successful assault. The reserves moving on behind will strengthen and hold all supporting points in rear of the attack.

If a successful assault is delivered, the assaulting troops will at once come under a converging artillery fire and be liable to counter-attack. The moment is critical, and every effort must be made to re-form the ranks and dispose the troops to hold the ground gained.

Such, in outline, might be the various stages of an infantry attack over such ground under present-day conditions.

Wood fighting and attacking through woods

Woerth is prolific in instruction on the subject of wood fighting, and brings into prominence the difficulties entailed and the characteristics and training of the troops necessary for success.

The advance of the 4th Bavarian Division through the Langensultzbach wood, and their ineffectual efforts to cross the clearing and drive the French from the northern edge of the Froeschweiler wood, have already been recounted in some detail. Many mistakes were made that might have been avoided. The officers of the 7th Brigade either could not read their maps or mistook the spire of Neehweiler church for that of Froeschweiler, and entered the wood in the wrong direction. The brigade was deployed on much too broad a front for adequate control to be maintained while moving through such an extensive wood. When fire was heard to the southeast the troops thought that their rear was threatened, and at once swung to their left. By the time they arrived at the south-west corner of the wood and came under fire all cohesion had been lost. When eventually a firing line was formed on the edge of the wood the units were much mixed up. It was impossible to exercise control, and no concerted effort could be made to advance across the clearing. The partial efforts of a few hundred men all failed, no doubt on account of the superiority of the French fire. There was no artillery support, and when counter-attacked on the flank, the troops gave way in disorder. The line was unduly extended, and there were no supports in rear of it.

It may be that the Bavarian troops were neither so well trained, nor so well commanded, nor such stubborn fighters as either the Prussians or the French, but, making due allowance for any inferiority in their fighting capacity, the operation which they attempted to undertake was one of exceptional difficulty. Infantry Training lays down that "when a wood intervenes between an attacking force and the defenders it may serve as a useful avenue of approach provided it is possible to deploy on the far side without exposure to fire at effective range. When, however, the attackers on reaching the far side come at once under the effective fire of the defence, they suffer from considerable disadvantages. It may be difficult to deploy in the wood, to maintain control, and to arrange a concerted effort for a further advance. Artillery may be unable to assist, and it may be difficult to find supporting positions in the event of counter-attack. In such circumstances the advantages of a covered approach may be overbalanced by these disadvantages, and it may be better to seek another line of advance."

Bonnal is of opinion that the approach march through the wood was very faultily conducted, that too large a proportion of the force was deployed, in the first instance, on too broad a front, that the first step should have been to occupy Langensultzbach securely, and that an advanced guard should have been utilized, the first objective of the attack being the north-east corner of the Froeschweiler wood. He sums up his comments as follows:–

> An approach march through a wood may be very dangerous if the flanks are not well protected.
>
> The dispositions should be similar to those that are suitable for night operations.
>
> Troops that advance through a wood in approach formation should be of excellent quality.

> The companies deployed on the edge of a wood are never in hand, and it seems to be necessary to assemble them before launching them in the open against an enemy that faces them.
>
> The direction of a fight on the edge of a wood is difficult, owing to the almost inevitable mixing of units.
>
> The edge of a wood favours the defence if it is a question of repelling an attack that is insufficiently prepared or is feeble.
>
> Woods inspire an instinctive fear in the attacker, even when they are only lightly defended, for the man who attacks dreads above all the danger which he suspects but does not see.
>
> Finally, history has not yet recorded a single great attack which has debouched from a forest or an extensive wood.
>
> This is not surprising, for if woods are extremely valuable for approach marches which precede engagements on the whole extent of the front of battle, they only exceptionally permit of the intimate combination of the three arms, without which it is not possible to prepare or to produce decisive results.[6]

The fighting in the Niederwald and the Froeschweiler wood shows the value of opposing an advance through a wood in order to break up an attack before it debouches. The opposition offered by the 3rd Zouaves to the greatly superior forces of the XIth Corps in the Niederwald completely disorganized the infantry of that corps, deprived it of offensive power for some time, and left it in a condition that invited counter-attack. The resistance offered by the 2nd Turcos and other units to the Ist Bavarians in the Froeschweiler wood prevented all but a small portion of the troops of that corps debouching from the wood and taking part in the attack on Froeschweiler.

The French have claimed considerable superiority in this form of fighting, particularly for their Algerian troops, the Zouaves and Turcos, and their claim appears to be fully justified. They attribute their superiority to the fact that these troops had considerable experience of fighting, and that they were consequently self-reliant, resourceful, and imbued with initiative. They had been trained to fight in groups, and men that became separated from their own companies or sections rallied to any officer or non-commissioned officer in whose neighbourhood they happened to find themselves. They, moreover, constantly assumed the offensive, and made good use of the bayonet as well as of the rifle.

Surely there are valuable lessons to be learnt from these incidents that are applicable at the present day. The value of the long range of modern weapons must be considerably reduced in wood fighting, and that of the bayonet correspondingly enhanced.

Counter-attack

Though no great counterstroke by a force kept in hand for the purpose, and designed to win the battle, took place at Woerth, few battles are more prolific in instances of local counter-attacks. The first point to consider in connexion with them is their nature and object, and the second their method of execution.

Assuming the crest of the Froeschweiler ridge to be the main French position, all the counterattacks were made in front of this position. The great majority were made to keep the enemy at a distance from it, to drive back his attack, in fact, before it could get to close

6. Author's translation.

grips with the main line of defence. A minority were made to cover the withdrawal of beaten troops, such as Lartigue's counter-attack on the Albrechtshauserhof, the counter-attack of the 1st Turcos, and the two cavalry charges.

Such counter-attacks as the majority of those delivered by the French use up the attacker's troops and draw fresh troops into the fight, but they also use up the troops of the defence, which, if we are to judge from Woerth, as a rule suffer heavily in withdrawing, particularly if they are courageous and press their attacks too far. If the French counter-attacks used up every available man of the Vth Corps, it must be admitted that they also exhausted MacMahon's reserves.

There is another type of local counter-attack, namely, that which is reserved till the enemy captures an important tactical point in the position, when it is launched for the limited purpose of recapturing the point that has been lost. Or, if the enemy penetrates between two tactical points and is thereby threatening to envelop one or both, a counter-attack may be launched to prevent such penetration or envelopment.

The French recognize the distinction and give different names, to the two types-namely, "contre-attaque" and, "retour offensif."

Our Field Service Regulations advocate both types. Local counter-attacks will be made to "drive back the enemy's firing line so that the enemy may be forced to use up his reserves to restore the battle;" and, again, "if an enemy succeeds in penetrating the position at any point a local counter-attack should be launched against him."

The former type is the more strongly emphasized of the two, yet we seldom or never practise it. What is the reason? Can it be that we are instinctively sceptical of its value under modern conditions?

There is no question on which it is more difficult to extract the true lessons of Woerth than this question of the value of the local counter-attack, delivered in front of the main position for the purpose of using up the enemy's reserves. The exhausting process was on this occasion reciprocal, and the French cannot be said to have gained any advantage from many of their local counterstrokes. The unanimous opinion of all commentators consulted by the writer is that they would have done better to have husbanded their reserves for the assumption of the offensive in greater force in a direction that would have been more telling.

Counter-attacks to cover the withdrawal of beaten troops are a necessity, but the employment of the whole available cavalry force for this purpose raises questions which will be discussed later.

The method of execution of the French counter-attacks must now be referred to. As a rule, the troops formed line and advanced till within full view of the enemy at short range, when they fired a volley or two and charged with the bayonet. The front line was seldom supported by a second line, and artillery support was usually wanting. The attacks were nearly all frontal, the troops were impetuous and followed up too far, losing heavily in withdrawing, and nothing but a local and temporary success was gained.

One of the best of these counter-attacks will be described in some detail as an example, namely, that delivered by Lartigue's Division against the portion of the advanced guard of the XIth Corps which crossed the Sauer by the Gunstett bridge.

At 9.30 a.m. the 2nd battalion, 50th Regiment, belonging to the 17th Corps, which had been on outpost, was reinforced by the 11th Chasseurs of the advanced guard of the XIth Corps. These two battalions engaged the 1st Chasseurs (French), which lined the high road, in a fire fight across the river. At 10 a.m. the 11th Chasseurs crossed the bridge, covered by the fire of 4 batteries on Gunstett Hill and of the 50th Regiment, and advanced to the attack of the 1st Chasseurs. Owing to the superiority of the German artillery, the French gave way in the direction of the Albrechtshauserhof, followed by the Germans. Lartigue then directed the 1st battalion 3rd Turcos and 2 companies, 2nd battalion, 3rd Turcos, to descend the Morsbronn ridge and attack the enemy's left flank. The 1st Chasseurs turned about and assumed the offensive at the same time, the whole movement being supported by 2 battalions 56th Regiment in second line. Being under a heavy artillery fire, which their own artillery was powerless to subdue, each battalion formed in line, and escaped heavy casualties from this cause. The Germans retired in great disorder over the bridge followed by 200 or 300 Turcos, who ran in pursuit of their adversaries towards Gunstett. The Turcos now came under a heavy fire from the 87th Regiment posted in the vineyards at the south-west corner of Gunstett Hill, and from the 80th Regiment in occupation of the outskirts of the village, and were obliged to retire suffering heavily. They re-crossed the bridge, but held on for some time in the hop gardens in its neighbourhood.

This counter-attack was admirable as regards the combination of the frontal and flank attacks, the support of a second line, and the suitability of the formations adopted. Efficient artillery support was unfortunately wanting, and the Turcos were too impetuous – they should have contented themselves with driving the enemy over the river. Troops that have been hunted back, as the 11th Chasseurs were on this occasion, need not be reckoned with seriously for many hours.

The question arises, what modifications of method would be necessary at the present time? There is the same necessity for striking the flank, for depth and weight in the attack, and for artillery support, but we now rely primarily on fire and not on the bayonet. In comparison with an ordinary attack the front line would extend less, the rushes would be quicker and longer, the pauses for fire shorter, and the supports would be closer up and would reinforce and carry the front line on at the slightest check. The whole movement must be carried through with rapidity, confidence, and dash, or it will very probably fail.

Employment of artillery

There can be no question that the methods employed by the German artillery at Woerth with so much success require considerable modification at the present day. We have reached, therefore, the realm of speculation, and in this connexion there is comparatively little to be learnt from the lessons of the battle that is applicable to our own time. It is true that the necessity for the close co-operation of the artillery and infantry is as imperative as ever, but the methods by which it is attained differ widely in many essential details.

The German artillery had failed in 1866, and great attention had subsequently been paid to questions of artillery tactics. The theory that had been evolved by the German General Staff may be summed up as follows:–

Artillery marched well forward in the columns. They deployed early in the greatest possible strength. The batteries advanced simultaneously into action and opened fire simultaneously.

The first object was to use the full force of the artillery mass to overwhelm the enemy's artillery in an artillery duel. If the enemy opposed a similar artillery mass it must be destroyed; if not, each portion of the enemy's artillery must be engaged by superior force and destroyed in turn. When this had been accomplished, the guns would be free to prepare and support the infantry attack.

These tactics were well suited to the artillery of the time, which, it must be borne in mind, used black powder, and had to see over the sights to develop effective fire. To see, in fact, was to be seen. They were exemplified by the artillery of the Vth Corps at Woerth, though it must be admitted somewhat imperfectly. As we have seen, the batteries could not deploy and advance simultaneously into action, owing to the heavy state of the ground. They advanced down the Dieffenbach-Woerth road and turned off to either side, taking three-quarters of an hour to get into action. As the enemy did not employ the tactics of the artillery mass, they were not in a position to take advantage of this somewhat dilatory deployment. The French had only one brigade of artillery with each division, of which one battery was armed with machine guns. The remainder were called Reserve Artillery, and only 6 batteries of the Reserve deployed against the massed batteries of the Vth Corps.

The German guns were able to concentrate their fire in turn on the different groups of the French artillery, and naturally got the best of the encounter. After 40 minutes of this unequal contest the French guns withdrew, but it must be noted that they were not by any means destroyed. According to the French Official History, the Commander of the Reserve Artillery realized that it would not serve any useful purpose to prolong the duel, and he was afraid that he would run short of ammunition before the infantry fight began in earnest. He accordingly ordered the batteries to retire, and they were subsequently able to intervene again and again in the action.

Although but imperfectly exemplified, it must be admitted that the tactics of the massed artillery had been fully justified. The German guns now dominated the situation in the centre of the battlefield, and were able to render the further interventions of the French artillery of comparatively little account, and to devote their attention to the support of their infantry or to repelling the many counter-attacks of the French infantry.

If these tactics were so successful, why should they be discarded? The answer is that the improvements in modern artillery have profoundly modified the conditions. The range and rapidity of fire of the guns have been greatly increased, smokeless powder enables guns to remain concealed when in action, and appliances for indirect laying enable effective fire to be developed from behind cover against all but rapidly moving targets. If the battle were to be fought again, and the Germans were to employ the same tactics, the result would be very different: The German guns, while fully exposed, would have no clearly defined target. The French would deploy a sufficient number of batteries for their purpose under cover of the Froeschweiler ridge, and, while practically immune from effective fire themselves, would very soon make matters extremely hot for the Germans. The latter would be fortunate if their gunners were not driven from their guns, and. if many of their pieces were not destroyed by direct hits. Far from being able to dominate the field and devote themselves to the task of supporting their own infantry, the massed batteries would be shortly either reduced to impotence, or using their fire exclusively for their own protection.

A change of method has, therefore, been dictated by the changed conditions. The early deployment, the simultaneous advance, the simultaneous opening of fire, the massed batteries and the artillery duel as a separate act have dropped out, and in their place we have substituted a much closer association between the artillery and infantry from the very start of the action; and we have adopted the principle of economy of force. The infantry, by advancing, must compel the enemy to disclose his position, while the artillery must be prepared to support the infantry with their fire at every stage of the action. We do not employ more guns than are necessary for our purpose, and if a greater volume of fire is required it is obtained by increasing the rate of fire, rather than by using more guns. We keep our fire power in hand.

The difference of method will be more clearly understood if we endeavour to follow the course of some incident of the battle as if it were being fought under the conditions of the present day. We will take again the attack of the 20th Brigade on the Galgenberg, as it will serve our purpose, and the reader who has followed the previous description of the infantry fire fight will be familiar with the ground over which the infantry must move.

We will assume, for the sake of convenience, that the operation is to be carried out by a British division instead of a German corps, and that the General Staff Officer of the division has ordered the artillery of the division to assemble in positions of readiness under cover of the Dieffenbach ridge, instead of ordering them into action. The General Officer commanding the division arrives on the ridge and decides to attempt to occupy the Galgenberg with the 20th Brigade for similar motives to those that have been attributed to Von Kirchbach.

The infantry will move in two columns via Woerth and Spachbach as already suggested, the Woerth column taking as its objective the northern end of the spur, and the Spachbach column taking the southern end (*see Map VII and Panorama*).

The Divisional Commander will allot the task of supporting this attack to what he considers to be a sufficient force of artillery for the purpose. The infantry being numerically weak for their task we will suppose that the General Officer Commanding decides to employ a strong force of artillery to support them, say 2 Q.F. Brigades and 1 battery of howitzers. Field Artillery Training lays down that the troops carrying out a distinct tactical task should be under one commander. The attack of the Galgenberg, in the conditions that we are assuming, is obviously a distinct tactical task, that is distinct from the operations of the IInd Bavarians or of the advanced guard of the XIth Corps. We will assume, therefore, that the commander of the 20th Infantry Brigade (General A) is placed in command of all the troops taking part in the operation, and that an artillery officer (Colonel X) is told off to command the 2 Brigades of Q.F. artillery and the howitzer battery that are to co-operate. These troops now form a "temporary group" under General A with a definite task allotted to them, namely to gain a footing on the Galgenberg and drive the enemy back from that position on Elsasshausen. According to Field Artillery Training, it now becomes the duty of Colonel X to seek out General A, and to find out from him the exact nature of the operation and the method of its execution.

Let us suppose that they meet on the Dieffenbach ridge, and that the following conversation takes place.

GENERAL A – I am going to attack in two columns, one by Woerth and the other by Spachbach. The Spachbach column will start first, as it has further to go, and has on the whole the more difficult task. It will move through the Fuchshübel wood and will endeavour to establish ½ battalion and the machine gun sections of 2 battalions on the line of the Spachbach-Goersdorf road. As soon as they debouch from the Fuchshübel wood they will be exposed to artillery fire from the Froeschweiler ridge. They will get down the hill as quickly as they can, and I want you to support them. That will be your first task. What can you do?

COLONEL X – I will do my best, but you will understand that, if the enemy's batteries remain completely concealed, I may be able to do very little. I will watch carefully for flashes or dust and do what I can to locate the enemy's guns or his observation posts. If an aeroplane reconnaissance could be made it might be of great assistance. I may add that if the enemy's batteries remain completely concealed, and your infantry move quickly, they probably won't suffer very heavily. If the guns come up to the crest I will give them a warm time.

GENERAL A – Very well. Now the next task will be to support the advance of the Woerth column in a similar manner through the zone swept by the enemy's artillery fire. They will deploy under cover of the Dieffenbach ridge on either side of the road and move straight on Woerth as rapidly as possible. When they reach Woerth they will get cover.

COLONEL X – My previous remarks apply equally to this column. I will get into touch with the column so that I shall know when it is about to start.

GENERAL A – When the Spachbach column reaches the village, the engineers must prepare some bridges. The enemy's artillery are sure to try and interfere, and long range rifle fire from the south-east corner of the Galgenberg may be nasty. Also, look out for the edge of the Niederwald. The situation there is rather uncertain.

COLONEL X – I understand.

GENERAL A – When the bridges are ready, the infantry will cross the river and try to rush across the meadows to the line of the railway. It is essential that you should know when this is about to take place. If you will arrange for communication with the Spachbach column, I will run a telephone to you from the Woerth column.

COLONEL X – I can do that, and will send an officer forward with the Spachbach column to keep me fully informed.

GENERAL A – I shall go with the Woerth column and establish a fireposition on the western outskirts of the village. As soon as I see that the Spachbach column has established itself on the line of the Hagenau high road, I shall endeavour to join hands with it and make a concerted advance up the hill. It is essential that my flanks should be protected, and I expect to suffer from fire from the edge of the Niederwald and from guns, and possibly machine guns, at the heads of the re-entrants. Please help me here if you can.

COLONEL X – I will do everything I can. I may be able to locate the guns at the heads of the re-entrants by their flashes, as they will quite possibly be firing direct, but the machine guns will be a difficult matter.

GENERAL A – I have not sufficient force to make my attack enveloping to any great extent, and it seems to me that the easiest line of approach will be against the western slopes of the spur. There I shall be defiladed from the enemy's artillery fire, and I trust to you largely to keep the enemy back from the forward crest, so that I shall be able to advance up the hill for some distance in dead ground.

COLONEL X – That will be my primary object when I see the infantry pressing forward up the hill.

GENERAL A – If I am successful in gaining a footing on the hill, I think it more than likely that I shall come under a heavy artillery fire as soon as I reach the crest, and that I shall be counterattacked. Now I want to ask you a question. Will you push guns forward during the attack, and will you be in a position to get any guns up on to the hill to help me when I get there?

COLONEL X – I do not think I can improve matters by pushing guns forward during the attack. The range from the crest of the Dieffenbach ridge is suitable, and the observation should be fairly easy. If I send the guns forward they will be exposed to the enemy's artillery fire for no adequate advantage. As regards getting guns forward to help you as soon as you gain a footing on the spur, I am afraid the Woerth road will be denied to me. It is fully exposed to the enemy's artillery fire, and I could hardly expect to get any number of guns down it. The only practicable route by which guns can reach the Galgenberg seems to me to be via Gunstett bridge and the Hagenau high road. It is a long detour, and of course could not be successfully undertaken till we have a secure hold on the Niederwald. On the whole, I suggest that I try and dribble a few guns forward through Woerth, a section at a time, as opportunity offers, and that I rely chiefly on flanking fire for supporting you against counterattack. If my guns are well dispersed, the enemy will be forced on to a very narrow front if he is to escape from the effects of my fire.

GENERAL A – I agree. Now where will you put your batteries?

COLONEL X – I have already suggested a fairly wide dispersion of the guns for one reason, but it seems to me important for another, namely, to get the full value of cross fire on your main objective, the Galgenberg. I suggest that 1 Q.F. Brigade be north of the Woerth-Dieffenbach road, that 2 Q.F. batteries and the howitzer battery be between the road and Fuchshübel wood, and that 1 Q.F. battery be south of Fuchshübel wood. Of course, fire from Gunstett Hill would enfilade the enemy's position to a large extent, but I do not propose to send a battery there. Some batteries of the XIth Corps are already established there, and I suggest that a request be sent through the General Officer Commanding the division to the XIth Corps, asking for some guns to co-operate with the attack on the Galgenberg from Gunstett Hill. I admit that you will have no control over them, and that from want of knowledge of what your object is they may conceivably do more harm than good at the critical moment, Still, I think the value of the cross fire is worth the risk, From the positions I have suggested I think I can carry out all the tasks you have referred to, but I will keep some guns in hand for unforeseen contingencies. That is to say, they will all be in action (under cover, to start with at any rate), but I shall not necessarily use the fire of all the guns at first.

GENERAL A – I agree with your proposals, but I am a bit afraid about those guns on Gunstett Hill, and I don't think I shall ask for support from that direction, at any rate at present.

After this conversation, which let us hope, between officers inspired with the same ideas, would not take anything like so long in reality as it takes to read, the artillery commander goes off to reconnoitre for positions for his batteries. The reconnaissance of the actual positions in this case should not present any considerable difficulty, and the artillery commander will be able to concentrate his attention on the communications between himself and his batteries, and between himself and the infantry. He must also choose his own position with care and with reference to that of his batteries. Having settled these preliminaries, he must allot tasks to his batteries, which will vary according to the progress made by the infantry. We will assume that the operation takes place as planned. The tasks will be as follows:–

1st Task

1st Q.F. Brigade (north of road). Watch for enemy's guns in the zone north of Woerth-Froeschweiler road.

2nd Q.F. Brigade (south of road). Watch for enemy's guns in the zone between Woerth-Froeschweiler road and Elsasshausen.
Battery south of Fuchshübel. In observation; no task allotted.
Howitzer Battery. Watch for enemy's guns south of Elsasshausen.
Woerth column reaches Woerth, Spachbach column reaches line Spachbach-Woerth road, and engineers begin to make bridges.

2nd Task

Zones for artillery targets as before.
Additional tasks – 2nd Q.F. Brigade keep down long range rifle fire from Galgenberg.
Battery south of Fuchshübel. Watch the Niederwald.
Information received from Spachbach column that the infantry are about to cross bridges and try and gain the line of the railway.

3rd Task

1st Brigade and howitzer battery. As before.
2nd Brigade, 2 batteries north of Fuchshübel wood. Keep down infantry fire from the Galgenberg.
Battery south of Fuchshübel wood. Keep down infantry fire from Niederwald and the re-entrants of Galgenberg.
Infantry now debouching from Woerth, and moving forward on the left to the line of the Hagenau high road.

4th Task

Artillery targets as before.
1st Q.F. Brigade. Protect flank of Woerth column from fire from the Froeschweiler re-entrant, and keep down fire of defenders of northern portion of Galgenberg.
2nd Q.F. Brigade. As before.
Howitzers. Neutralize artillery and turn on to any trenches on Galgenberg.
Infantry nearing summit of Galgenberg and preparing to assault.

5th Task

No change of tasks, but fire on Galgenberg increased in intensity.
Successful assault delivered, but attackers come under heavy artillery fire, and hostile infantry move forward from Elsasshausen to counterattack. Attempt to get a section of guns through Woerth failed.

6th Task

Artillery targets as before, but majority of guns turned on to counter-attack.
1st Q.F. Brigade. Counter-attack north of Elsasshausen-Woerth road.
2nd Q.F. Brigade. Counter-attack south of Elsasshausen-Woerth road.
Infantry give way before counter-attack.

7th Task

All Brigades fire on Galgenberg to prevent enemy reaching crest to pursue infantry with fire, but care must be taken not to superimpose the fire of batteries so that they cannot distinguish their projectiles.

It has been assumed that the action took the form foreseen by General A, but nothing in war ever happens exactly as expected. While, therefore, it is always desirable to have a clear plan, to know exactly what you are trying to do, and to persevere to the utmost in the attempt to carry the plan through, it is very undesirable to make plans too far ahead, and it is essential to be prepared to meet unforeseen contingencies. This applies with force to artillery tactics. We do not commit our full strength till it is required – we unfold it, so to speak, as we go along.

We will now suppose that after this repulse the Divisional Commander decides to use the full strength of his division in driving back the enemy's advanced troops, and attempting to gain the line Froeschweiler-Elsasshausen. The infantry brigade, that has already been engaged, will not be in a condition to resume the offensive for some time, so the two remaining brigades will deploy supported by the whole of the artillery of the division. We will suppose that the Dieffenbach-Woerth-Froeschweiler road is the dividing line between the two brigades. Including the battalions already engaged, there will thus be 8 battalions operating south of the road, and 4 north of it. Now Field Artillery Training says that when the whole of the troops of a division are taking part in an operation under the direct control of the divisional commander, the system of "temporary grouping" of infantry and artillery that has just been described will not, as a, rule, be resorted to. That is to say, the artillery will not come under the direct orders of the subordinate infantry commanders with whom they are co-operating, but will be under the orders of the C.R.A. of the division. That is the case that we are now dealing with, and the mission of the 20th. Infantry Brigade having ended, owing to the failure of the attack, the "temporary group" originally formed should be broken up, and the artillery that had been under the General Officer Commanding 20th Infantry Brigade should revert to the control of the C.R.A. That officer will now select positions for the whole of the artillery of the division, and allot tasks to the several brigades, in accordance with the instructions of the divisional commander.

Space does not permit of entering into further details, but the C.R.A. will probably allot to certain artillery brigades the primary tasks of supporting the attacks on Froeschweiler and Elsasshausen respectively. Field Artillery Training makes it quite clear that in such a case the subordinate artillery commander must confer with the subordinate infantry commander with whom he is to co-operate in the manner that has already been described, even though he is not placed directly under his orders. Communication between the two arms will also be kept up throughout the operation, whether the system of "temporary grouping" is adopted or not. In this manner, the close co-operation of the artillery is assured, and, at the same time, the C.R.A. is in a position to allot secondary tasks to his brigades, which allows him to make full use of cross and converging fire, when the circumstances are such that these can be used with effect.

We will now turn to the employment of the artillery of the XIth Corps. It is hardly necessary to point out that 72 guns could not be concentrated on Gunstett Hill under the conditions of the present day. Owing to the configuration of the ground it is most difficult to conceal artillery on this hill. Guns on the north of the hill are exposed to view from the Froeschweiler ridge, and guns to the south are exposed to view from the Morsbronn ridge. Moreover, the massing of the bulk of the artillery on this hill would sacrifice the very great advantage of a converging artillery fire in support of an enveloping attack. Everything, therefore, points to the desirability of a wide dispersion of the artillery on this flank, as far as and even beyond Durrenbach, if adequate escort can be provided. It is clear that the attack of the Morsbronn ridge is a distinct tactical operation, and that the troops taking part in it should be under one commander. They would not, therefore, be subdivided into "temporary groups," and the artillery would remain under the control of a single artillery commander. The desirability of this is clear if we consider the tasks which the artillery would be called upon to carry out. Supposing a "temporary group" were formed to operate, as did Von Schkopp's column, via Durrenbach on Morsbronn, the artillery of that group would support the attack on Morsbronn certainly, but if it confined itself to this task the value of a converging and partially enfilade fire against the defenders of the Albrechtshauserhof and the slopes of the Morsbronn ridge would be sacrificed. The allotment of tasks by the C.R.A. so as to make full use of converging fire is, therefore, of paramount importance in this case.

As regards the defence generally, there are three main positions available for artillery – the head of the clearing, the Froeschweiler-Elsasshausen ridge, and the Morsbronn ridge. There is not much need or scope for artillery in the defence of the left flank. A brigade suitably posted to flank the clearing and prevent the enemy debouching from the Langensultzbach wood is probably all that could be usefully employed. West of the Froeschweiler ridge there are suitable positions for concealed batteries which could be used to delay the advance of the hostile infantry down the slopes of the Dieffenbach ridge, and to engage the enemy's artillery. There are also excellent positions at the heads of the re-entrants from which to flank the spurs, prevent the enemy debouching from Woerth, building bridges over the Sauer, and crossing the meadows.

The Morsbronn ridge affords good concealed positions facing east from which to prevent the enemy debouching from Gunstett and crossing the river and meadows. But; when once the enemy's infantry reach the foot of the ridge, artillery co-operation with the defence becomes very difficult, owing to the command of Gunstett Hill, which allows the enemy a full view of any guns that are run forward to the crest. The artillery on this part of the position would nowadays probably compel the turning movement to move on a very wide arc, possibly even forcing the enemy to enter the Hagenau forest. As the turning movement developed, artillery on the Forstheim ridge would be invaluable, and this position would be essential for the support of, any counter-attack delivered against the enemy's left flank before it gained access to the Niederwald.

Employment of cavalry

The Crown Prince's orders to the 4th Cavalry Division for the 6th August were to remain in bivouac at Shoenenburg, about 8 miles east of Woerth. The sound of the guns at Woerth was audible at Shoenenburg from an early hour, but Prince Albert of Prussia, who commanded the division, considered it to be consistent with his duty to remain in bivouac and await orders. Instead of saddling up and getting the division ready to move, while he reported personally to Army Headquarters for instructions, he remained with his troops and sent orderly officers to ask for orders. Unfortunately, the Headquarter Staff was so immersed in the events of the battle that the Cavalry Division was forgotten till a late hour in the evening, and the orderly officers "did not find an opportunity" to speak to anybody in authority. The result was the complete inaction of the Cavalry Division throughout the course of the battle, nor was the division in a position to take part in the pursuit.

The question arises, what use should and could have been made of the Cavalry Division? Cavalry Training says that before a battle cavalry should be concentrated in positions of readiness. "In selecting these it is essential to study the configuration of the ground and its cavalry capacity, and to endeavour to foresee the nature of the fighting ... whenever possible the bulk of the cavalry should usually be on that flank which offers the greatest freedom of movement." Such considerations point to the move of the 4th Cavalry Division at an early hour to Surburg, with a view to co-operation with the XIth Corps in the envelopment of the French right flank. The country between Morsbronn and the Hagenau forest was suitable for the action of cavalry, and the presence of a strong cavalry force in the neighbourhood of Gundershoffen during the afternoon might have had far-reaching results. Energetic action might well have led to the enemy being driven off his line of retreat on Saverne, and being compelled to fall back by Niederbronn on Bitche, or disperse in the Vosges mountains.

The inactivity of the corps cavalry is more easily understood, as the actual battlefield was certainly unsuitable for cavalry action. But in the absence of the 4th Cavalry Division, it would still have been possible for a considerable force of cavalry to concentrate on the left flank in sufficient time to be most usefully employed, if thought had been given to the matter at Army Headquarters.

The feebleness of the pursuit is not, therefore, altogether accounted for by the absence of the Cavalry Division.

The French cavalry are not open to the charge of remaining ingloriously inactive, though their employment is open to criticism. The heroism with which they sacrificed themselves in order to cover the withdrawal of the infantry has been recorded, but could they not have been put to a more useful purpose without the necessity for such sacrifices?

Controversy has raged round this question of the employment of cavalry in battle during the past ten years in this country with much bitterness, but for a short time there appears to have been a truce, and the views of the General Staff, as embodied in Field Service Regulations and Cavalry Training, are now less frequently attacked. Those views are that the primary duty of cavalry in battle is to make use of the opportunities produced by the other arms, and that those opportunities will be likely to occur as the crisis of the battle is reached. Cavalry, therefore, should be suitably placed to take advantage of these opportunities, and the cavalry commander should take every possible step to inform himself of the progress of events, so that he may intervene with decisive effect when the opportunity offers.

If we endeavour to apply this doctrine to the French cavalry at the battle of Woerth by the light of the passage quoted above from Cavalry Training, it appears reasonable to suggest that MacMahon should have concentrated the bulk of his cavalry west of the Forstheim ridge, with the object of co-operating on the outer flank of his General Reserve in a counterstroke against the flank of the XIth Corps. In this position the cavalry would have had freedom of movement, and could have gained access to ground suitable to their action. The resistance offered by Lartigue's Division, coupled with the counter-attack of the General Reserve, would, in all probability, have produced an opportunity for the employment of a considerable cavalry force with decisive results. In the opinion of the General Staff these results can still be obtained in favourable circumstances by shock action.

It will be remembered that the employment of the German 4th Cavalry Division on the same flank has been recommended. At first sight it may appear that in such a case the two cavalry forces would either neutralize one another with dismounted action, or engage in a cavalry encounter such as took place on the 16th August, 1870, near Ville sur Yron. It must be admitted that such results are not unlikely, but cavalry encounters wide on the flank of a battle should not be sought after for their own sake, and the action of the cavalry should be reserved for those opportunities that are likely to produce the most decisive results.

The cavalry of the defence has an important function to perform in these days in hampering and delaying the turning movement with dismounted fire. A Brigade of cavalry in the valley of the Eberbach, trained as our cavalry now are in the use of the rifle, and supported by artillery from the Forstheim ridge, would have made things very unpleasant for Von Schkopp in the absence of any strong force of cavalry supporting the turning movement.

It is impossible to leave the subject of cavalry without a further reference to the charge of Michel's unfortunate Cuirassiers, which has so often been quoted by the opponents of shock action in support of their arguments. When considering the value of such arguments based on this incident we must remember the facts. No previous reconnaissance, a commander taken by surprise and not aware of the situation that he was called upon to deal with, haste and consequent confusion, a very unsuitable terrain, the worst possible direction chosen, and, finally, a village taken as an objective. Some excellent authorities think that if Michel had been better informed as to the situation and the ground, had moved down the valley of the Eberbach under cover and, forming to the left, had charged Von Schkopp's infantry in flank instead of in front, he might have achieved great results. No doubt by these means surprise might have been achieved, and, when that is the case, all things are possible. Even the most sceptical will probably admit that if the French cavalry commander had been imbued with the spirit of our present regulations, and had acted up to them, he might have used his nine squadrons with far greater effect and less loss.

Strengthening supporting points and entrenching in the attack

The Germans in 1870 were, as a rule, careful to strengthen supporting points in rear of attacking troops, a very wise and a very necessary precaution. We know that they put Woerth in a state of defence, which assisted them in repelling many counter-attacks. We are told that at one time they set a battalion to work to strengthen a position on the Dieffenbach ridge. Probably these were not the only occasions on which they applied this important principle.

Such tactical points as Langensultzbach, the Oil Mill, the Saw Mill, Woerth, the line of the Hagenau high road, Spachbach, the Bruchmill, and Gunstett, should be occupied by reserve troops, and placed in a state of defence as soon as the position of the firing lines affords adequate protection to the working parties.

We do not, however, read of any entrenching taking place in the firing lines during the actual progress of the attack. To some extent this appears to be a comparatively new idea, based on the methods adopted by the Japanese in Manchuria, though we know that Skobeleff's troops, after their experiences before Plevna, carried their heavy entrenching tools on their backs to within a few miles of Constantinople rather than be parted from them.

When considering this question of entrenching in the attack, let us liken a battle for a moment to a boxing match. Some battles, like some boxing matches, are fought quickly, while others are fought slowly. The national characteristics of some troops, and the way that others are trained, tend to make them quick fighters, and to make others slow fighters. It would probably be right to say that the French would always be quick fighters. They certainly were at Woerth, and exhausted themselves rapidly in consequence. The Russians on the other hand would probably always be slow fighters.

These characteristics would naturally react on their opponents. Against such opponents as the French proved themselves to be at Woerth the Germans were obliged to force the pace in order to make their numerical superiority tell. The Japanese against a less active enemy could adopt more leisurely methods.

One has only to ask the question, where would the XIth Corps have been at 4 p.m. if the firing lines had stopped to entrench every vantage point gained, to realize that such methods are not suited to the task which fell to the lot of this corps. Too much spade work in the XIth Corps would not only have let off Lartigue's Division, but would have allowed MacMahon time to alter his dispositions and arrange an effective counterstroke. The battle could not have been won before dark.

While admitting then that the "attack with the shovel" may be a necessity under modern conditions in frontal attacks against strongly defended localities, it seems to be very desirable to remember that occasions will arise when time is of the utmost importance, and when, consequently, the adoption of such methods is entirely out of place. The necessity to force the pace of the decisive attack is as imperative as ever.

The fighting capacity of the troops

It is not possible to close this discussion without a reference to the fighting capacity of the troops engaged. "The moral is to the physical as three to one," said Napoleon.

History leaves us in little doubt as to the inferior fighting capacity of the Bavarian troops. Compulsory service was only introduced in Bavaria in 1867, and very naturally the Bavarian Army had not yet reaped the full benefits of this measure. An army cannot be made by the mere alteration of the law as to recruiting. Many reservists had received only the most elementary instruction, and both the system of training and the Training Regulations were inferior to those of the Prussian Army. The Bavarians had given but a poor account of themselves in 1866, and evidently their moral had not recovered. At Woerth their complete want of success, coupled with their casualty returns, is the best evidence of their inferiority.

The Prussian Army of. 1870 was highly organized, sternly disciplined, ably commanded, well staffed, well trained, and animated by an admirable offensive spirit. The achievements of the Vth and XIth Corps, and the losses they suffered, are eloquent testimony of their stubbornness and endurance in the attack. And yet here is the account[7] of a Prussian company commander of what he saw that day:–

> I recalled my first battle in France. We did not arrive on the field till late in the day. We crossed it where the battle had been fiercest. What a sight it was! I was already familiar with the sight of the dead and the mangled, and with the sound of the cries of the wounded, but not with what now met my eyes. The field was literally strewed with men who had left the ranks, and were doing nothing. Whole battalions could have been formed from them. From where we stood you could count hundreds. Some were lying down, their rifles pointing to the front, as if they were still in the firing line, and were expecting the enemy to attack them at any moment.

7. "A Summer Night's Dream" (usually attributed to Meckel) translated by Captain Gawne and published in the *U.S. Magazine*, 1890. Bonnal considers it indisputable that the reference is to Woerth.

> These had evidently remained behind, lying down, when the more courageous had advanced. Others had squatted like hares in the furrows. Wherever a bush or ditch gave shelter, there were men to be seen, who in some cases had made themselves very comfortable. All these men gazed at us without showing the least interest. The fact that we belonged to another army corps seemed to be a sufficient excuse for treating us with blank indifference. I heard them say: 'These fellows, like the others, are going to let themselves be shot.'
>
> During our advance, before we came under any really serious fire, and while only the whistle of an occasional stray bullet could be heard, we saw six men, one behind the other in a long queue, cowering at the back of a tree. Afterwards I saw this sight so often that I became accustomed to it. Who did not? At the time it was new to me. The tree I speak of was not thick enough to give cover even to one man. In this instance the sixth was a sergeant. Near the tree there were little irregularities of ground that would have given good cover to all six.

And these things happened to the most highly disciplined troops in Europe, when subjected to the strain of several hours' continuous fighting. Henderson is indeed right when he says "it is only by studying the records of the past that we can acquire a true idea of what we have to face in the future. How, when death reigns supreme, human nature is affected, to what extent training, discipline and habit may be relied on to counteract the instincts of self-preservation, how leading is to be carried on amid the excitement, the losses, and the din of battle, are questions of paramount importance, and no mere effort of the imagination will help to solve them. If we would learn what men can do, and what they cannot do, under stress of fire, we must turn to history."

Bonnal, who was present at the battle, admits that similar defections took place amongst the French troops. Officers who had to make their way through the woods at different times met many soldiers who were thinking of anything but how to rejoin their units and continue fighting. The soldiers of the Western nations are always men, and not necessarily brave men, whatever uniform they may wear, yet he records his opinion that defections from duty were more numerous amongst the Germans, at the beginning of the war, than amongst the old French regiments.

This is a matter which, as he says, "leads to a consoling idea, and introduces an element of hope," a sentiment in which we may perhaps be allowed to join.

It is the author's hope that no one will be able to read even this bald narrative without a thrill of admiration for the dash and energy in attack, and the stubborn refusal to accept defeat of the brave French troops who fought at Woerth and upheld so nobly the honour of their country and of their arms.

Chapter VII

After the Battle

The French retreat

The bulk of the fugitives from Woerth took the road via Bouxviller to Saverne, a few only going to Bitche. The cavalry reached Saverne between 2 a.m. and 4 a.m. on the 7th, but the infantry kept on arriving all through the forenoon, and were much exhausted, having marched throughout the night.

The last train to leave Strasburg reached Saverne at 5 p.m., and in the evening a false report that a strong German column had reached Steinburg, only a few miles north of Saverne, caused MacMahon to order the resumption of the retreat on Saarburg. This march completed the exhaustion of the already greatly fatigued infantry.

Lespart's Division of the Vth Corps reached Niederbronn at 5 p.m. on the 6th, and made dispositions to cover the retreat. At 7 o'clock the division retired in two columns, one towards Bitche and the other on Saverne. When De Failly heard of the result of the actions at Woerth and Spicheren, he ordered the remaining divisions of his corps to retire from Rohrbach and Bitche on Pfalzburg, taking the roads through the mountains, so as to avoid contact with the enemy if possible. If the divisions of this corps had made the same exertions to reach the battlefield of Woerth as they did to avoid pursuit when the battle was over, the result might have been altogether different.

From the neighbourhood of Saarburg the retreat of the Ist and Vth Corps, was, continued on Lunéville, and thence on Neufchateau and Chaumont, where the two corps entrained between the 14th and 16th August for Chalons.

The troops during this march suffered the greatest hardships owing to the ignorance of the French commanders and staff of the art of billeting and requisitioning. The men had taken off their equipment to fight, and their knapsacks had been abandoned in the retreat. The transport and supply services were completely disorganized, and the weather being wet the troops bivouacked night after night soaked to the skin, with no means of subsistence but plunder. It. was the "retreat from Moscow, without the snow," and the condition of the force on arrival at Chalons was pitiable in the extreme.

The German pursuit

The German army bivouacked in the neighbourhood of the battlefield on the night of the 6th, and the whole army rested on the 7th, with the exception of the Baden Division, which moved to Hagenau. Touch was lost with MacMahon's army, and the conclusion was arrived at that he would retire through the Vosges and effect a junction with the Emperor as soon as possible. The original plan of passing the Vosges was therefore adhered to, in order that the IIIrd Army might assemble on the Upper Saar, and so be in a position to attack the right flank of the French. The passage of the mountains was effected in five columns between the 8th and 12th August.

The columns were formed as follows from right to left:

IInd Bavarian Corps.

Ist Bavarian Corps.
Wurtemburg Division.
Vth Corps.
XIth Corps.

The Baden Division proceeded to invest Strasburg. The march was conducted by easy stages, and by the 12th August the IIIrd Army was assembled in the order named on the line Saarunion-Saarburg. But by this time events had moved forward in Lorraine. The Emperor, after Spicheren, had retreated on Metz, and the IIIrd Army, instead of being on the flank of the French, and in a position to co-operate in a general offensive, was now echeloned in rear of the left of the IInd Army at a considerable distance from any force of the enemy.

The art of rapid marching, combined with billeting in depth along the route selected, was as little understood at that time by the Germans as by the French.

Appendix I

Order of Battle of the French forces engaged at the Battle of Weissenburg

2nd Division: Général Douay

1st Brigade: Général Peletier de Montmarie
50th Line Regiment (3 battalions)
74th Line Regiment (3 battalions)
16th Chasseurs à Pied (1 battalion)

2nd Brigade: Général Pellé
78th Line Regiment (3 battalions)
1st Algerian Tirailleur Regiment (Turcos) (3 battalions)

Artillery
9/9th Artillery Regiment (6 guns)
12/9th Artillery Regiment (6 guns)
10/9th Artillery Regiment (6 Mitrailleuse)

1st Engineer Regiment (1 company)

1st Cavalry Brigade: Général de Septeuil (attached from Duhesme's Cavalry Division)
3rd Hussar Regiment (4 squadrons)
11th Chasseur à Cheval Regiment (4 squadrons)

Appendix II

Order of Battle of the German forces engaged at the Battle of Weissenburg

IInd Bavarian Corps, 4th Division (General von Bothmer)

7th Brigade (Col. Borries von Wissel)
5th Infantry (2 battalions)
9th Infantry (3 battalions)
6th Jäger Battalion

8th Brigade (Major General Maillinger)
3/1st Infantry
3/5th Infantry
1/7th Infantry
3/11th Infantry
3/14th Infantry
5th Jäger Battalion

Divisional Troops
10th Jäger Battalion
2nd Chevauxlegers
4th Artillery Regiment - 1 Division (4 batteries)

Vth Corps, 9th Division (Major General von Sandrart)

17th Brigade (Colonel von Bothmer)
58th Infantry (3 battalions)
59th Infantry (3 battalions)

18th Brigade (Colonel von Voights-Retz)
7th Grenadiers(3 battalions)
47th Infantry (3 battalions)

Divisional Troops
5th Jäger Battalion
4th Dragoons
5th Artillery Regiment, 1st Foot Division (4 batteries)

XIth Corps, 21st Division (Major General von Schachtmeyer)

41st Brigade (Colonel von Koblinski)
80th Fusiliers (3 battalions)
87th Infantry (3 battalions)

42nd Brigade (Major General von Thile)
82nd Infantry (3 battalions)
88th Infantry (3 battalions)

Divisional Troops
11th Jäger Battalion
14th Hussars
11th Artillery Regiment, 1st Foot Division (4 batteries)

Appendix III

Order of Battle of the French forces engaged at the Battle of Woerth

I Army Corps (Maréchal de MacMahon)

1st Division: Général Ducrot
1st Brigade: Général Wolff
18th Line Regiment (3 battalions)
96th Line Regiment (3 battalions)
13th Chasseurs à Pied (1 battalion)

2nd Brigade: Général de Postis du Houlbec
45th Line Regiment (3 battalions)
1st Zouave Regiment (3 battalions)

Artillery: Lt. Colonel Lecoeuvre
6/9th Artillery Regiment (6 guns)
7/9th Artillery Regiment (6 guns)
8/9th Artillery Regiment (6 Mitrailleuse)

1st Engineer Regiment (1 company)

2nd Division: Général Pellé
1st Brigade: Général Peletier de Montmarie
50th Line Regiment (3 battalions)
74th Line Regiment (3 battalions)
16th Chasseurs à Pied (1 battalion)

2nd Brigade: Général Pellé
78th Line Regiment (3 battalions)
1st Algerian Tirailleur Regiment (3 battalions)

Artillery
9/9th Artillery Regiment (6 guns)
12/9th Artillery Regiment (6 guns)
10/9th Artillery Regiment (6 Mitrailleuse)

1st Engineer Regiment (1 company)

3rd Division: Général Raoult

1st Brigade: Général L'Hériller

36th Line Regiment (3 battalions)
2nd Zouave Regiment (3 battalions)
8th Chasseurs à Pied (1 battalion)

2nd Brigade: Général Lefebvre

48th Line Regiment (3 battalions)
2nd Algerian Tirailleur Regiment (3 battalions)

Artillery: Lt. Colonel Cheguillaume

5/12th Artillery Regiment (6 guns)
6/12th Artillery Regiment (6 guns)
9/12th Artillery Regiment (6 Mitrailleuse)

1st Engineer Regiment (1 company)

4th Division: Général de Lartigue

1st Brigade: Général Fraboulet de Kerléader

56th Line Regiment (3 battalions)
3rd Zouave Regiment (3 battalions)
1st Chasseurs à Pied (1 battalion)

2nd Brigade: Général Lacretelle

3rd Algerian Tirailleur Regiment (3 battalions)
(87th Line Regiment absent)

Artillery: Lt. Colonel Lamandé

7/12th Artillery Regiment (6 guns)
11/12th Artillery Regiment (6 guns)
10/12th Artillery Regiment (6 Mitrailleuse)

1st Engineer Regiment (1 company)

Cavalry Division: Général Duhesme

1st Brigade: Général de Septeuil

3rd Hussar Regiment (4 squadrons)
11th Chasseur à Cheval Regiment (4 squadrons)

2nd Brigade: Général de Nansouty

10th Dragoon Regiment (4 squadrons)
2nd Lancer Regiment (4 squadrons)
4th Lancer Regiment (4 squadrons)

3rd Brigade: Général Michel
8th Cuirassier Regiment (4 squadrons)
9th Cuirassier Regiment (4 squadrons)

Corps Artillery Reserve: Colonel de Bassart
11/6th Artillery Regiment (6 guns)
12/6th Artillery Regiment (6 guns)
5/9th Artillery Regiment (6 guns)
11/9th Artillery Regiment (6 guns)
1/20th Horse Artillery Regiment (6 guns)
2/20th Horse Artillery Regiment (6 guns)
3/20th Horse Artillery Regiment (6 guns)
4/20th Horse Artillery Regiment (6 guns)

Engineering Reserve
1st Engineer Regiment (1½ companies)

Attached from VII Army Corps

1st Division: Général Conseil Dumesnil
1st Brigade: Général Nicolai
3rd Line Regiment (3 battalions)
21st Line Regiment (3 battalions)
17th Chasseurs à Pied (1 battalion)

2nd Brigade: Général Maire
47th Line Regiment (3 battalions)
99th Line Regiment (3 battalions)

Cavalry Division (Général de Bonnemains)

1st Brigade: Général Girard
1st Cuirassier Regiment (4 squadrons)
4th Cuirassier Regiment (4 squadrons)

2nd Brigade: Général de Brauer
2nd Cuirassier Regiment (4 squadrons)
3rd Cuirassier Regiment (4 squadrons)

Artillery: Chef d'escadron Astier
7/19th Horse Artillery Regiment (6 guns)
8/19th Horse Artillery Regiment (6 Mitrailleuse)

Appendix IV

Order of Battle of the German forces engaged at the Battle of Woerth

Vth Corps (Lieutenant General von Kirchbach)

9th Division (Major General von Sandrart)

17th Brigade (Colonel von Bothmer)
58th Infantry (3 battalions)
59th Infantry (3 battalions)

18th Brigade (Colonel von Voights-Retz)
7th Grenadiers(3 battalions)
47th Infantry (3 battalions)

Divisional Troops
5th Jäger Battalion
4th Dragoons
5th Artillery Regiment, 1st Foot Division (4 batteries)

10th Division (Major General von Schmidt)

19th Brigade (Colonel von Henning auf Schönhoff)
46th Infantry (3 battalions)
6th Grenadiers (3 battalions)

20th Brigade (Major General Walther von Monbary)
50th Regiment (3 battalions)
37th Fusiliers (3 battalions)

Divisional Troops
14th Dragoons
5th Artillery Regiment, 3rd Foot Division (4 batteries)

Corps Artillery (Lieutenant Colonel Köhler)
5th Artillery Regiment, Horse Artillery Battalion (2 batteries)
5th Artillery Regiment, 2nd Foot Division (4 batteries)

XIth Corps (Lieutenant General von Bose)

21st Division (Major General von Schachtmeyer)

41st Brigade (Colonel von Koblinski)
80th Fusiliers (3 battalions)
87th Infantry (3 battalions)

42nd Brigade (Major General von Thile)
82nd Infantry (2 battalions)
88th Infantry (3 battalions)

Divisional Troops
11th Jäger Battalion
14th Hussars
11th Artillery Regiment, 1st Foot Division (4 batteries)

22nd Division (Lieutenant General von Gersdorff)

43rd Brigade (Colonel von Kontzki)
95th Infantry (3 battalions)
32nd Infantry (3 battalions, less 1 company)

44th Brigade (Major General von Schkopp)
94th Infantry (3 battalions)
83rd Infantry (3 battalions)

Divisional Troops
13th Hussars
11th Artillery Regiment, 2nd Foot Division (4 batteries)

Corps Artillery (Colonel von Oppeln-Bronikowski)
11th Artillery Regiment, Horse Artillery Battalion (2 batteries)
11th Artillery Regiment, 3rd Foot Division (4 batteries)

1st Bavarian Infantry Division (Lieutenant General von Stephan)

Advanced Guard (2nd Infantry Brigade) (Major General von Orff)

Advance (Major Reschreiter, CO 4th Jäger Battalion)
4th Jäger Battalion
1/2nd Infantry
3rd Chevauxlegers (2 squadrons)

Main body of Advanced Guard (Colonel Count von Leublfing, CO 11th Infantry)
2 & 3/2nd Infantry
1 & 2/11th Infantry
3rd Chevauxlegers (1½ squadrons)
1st Artillery Regiment – 1 battery

Main body (1st Infantry Brigade) (Major General Dietl)
Leib Regiment (2 battalions, less 1 company)
1 & 2/1st Infantry
2nd Jäger Battalion
9th Jäger Battalion
3rd Chevauxlegers (½ squadron)
1st Artillery Regiment – 4 batteries

4th Bavarian Infantry Division (Lieutenant General Count von Bothmer)

Advanced Guard (7th Infantry Brigade) (Major General von Thiereck)

Advance (Major Caries, CO 6th Jäger Battalion)
6th Jäger Battalion
2nd Chevauxlegers (¼ squadron)

Main body of Advanced Guard (Colonel von Heeg, CO 9th Infantry)
1, 2 & 3/9th Infantry
2nd Chevauxlegers (2¾ squadrons)
4th Artillery Regiment – 1 battery

Left flanking detachment (Major Goës, CO 2/5th Infantry)
1 & 2/5th Infantry
2nd Chevauxlegers (1 squadron)

Main body (8th Infantry Brigade) (Major General Maillinger)
3/1st Infantry
3/5th Infantry
1/7th Infantry
3/11th Infantry
3/14th Infantry
10th Jäger Battalion
4th Artillery Regiment – 3 batteries

Attached from Reserve Artillery Division (Lieutenant Colonel Eckart)
2nd Artillery Regiment – 3 batteries

Attached from Lancer Brigade (Major General Baron von Muizer)[1]
5th Chevauxlegers (2 squadrons)
1st Lancers (4 squadrons)
2nd Artillery Regiment – 1 battery

Bavarian troops later brought forward

5th Infantry Brigade (Major General von Schleich)
1, 2 & 3/6th Infantry
2 & 3/7th Infantry
8th Jäger Battalion

Lancer Brigade (Major General Baron von Muizer)
5th Chevauxlegers (2 squadrons)
1st Lancers (4 squadrons)
2nd Lancers (4 squadrons)
2nd Artillery Regiment – 1 battery

Detached from 3rd Infantry Division
1st Chevauxlegers (2 squadrons)
4th Artillery Regiment – 1 battery

Württemberg Division (elements)

2nd Field Brigade (Major General von Starkloff)
1/2nd Infantry
2/2nd Infantry (2 companies only)
1 & 2/5th Infantry
3rd Jäger Battalion
2nd Foot Artillery Division (2 batteries)

Reserve cavalry (Major General Count von Schéler)
4th Cavalry (4 squadrons)
3rd Cavalry (1 squadron)

1 Elements of these formations appear for a second time, representing a more complete deployment of the Lancer Brigade.

BOOKS IN THIS SERIES:

1. *The Battle of Majuba Hill The Transvaal Campaign 1880–1881* John Laband (ISBN 978-1-911512-38-7)
2. *For Queen and Company Vignettes of the Irish Soldier in the Indian Mutiny* David Truesdale (ISBN 978-1-911512-79-0)
3. *The Furthest Garrison Imperial Regiments in New Zealand 1840–1870* Adam Davis (ISBN 978-1-911628-29-3)
4. *Victory Over Disease Resolving the Medical Crisis in the Crimean War, 1854–1856* Michael Hinton (ISBN 978-1-911628-31-6)
5. *Journey Through the Wilderness Garnet Wolseley's Canadian Red River Expedition of 1870* Paul McNicholls (ISBN 978-1-911628-30-9)
6. *Kitchener The Man Not The Myth* Anne Samson (ISBN 978-1-912866-45-8)
7. *The British and the Sikhs Discovery, Warfare and Friendship c1700–1900* Gurinder Singh Mann (ISBN 978-1-911628-24-8)
8. *Bazaine 1870 Scapegoat for a Nation* Quintin Barry (ISBN 978-1-913336-08-0)
9. *Redcoats in the Classroom The British Army's Schools For Soldiers and Their Children During the 19th Century* Howard R. Clarke (ISBN 978-1-912866-47-2)
10. *The Rescue They Called a Raid The Jameson Raid 1895–96* David Snape (ISBN 978-1-913118-77-8)
11. *Hungary 1848 The Winter Campaign* Christopher Pringle (ISBN 978-1-913118-78-5)
12. *The War of the Two Brothers The Portuguese Civil War 1828-1834* Sérgio Veludo Coelho (ISBN 978-1-914059-26-1)
14. *Forgotten Victorian Generals Studies in the Exercise of Command and Control in the British Army 1837–1901* Christopher Brice (editor) (ISBN 978-1-910777-20-6)
15. *The German War of 1866 The Bohemian and Moravian Campaign* Theodore Fontane (ISBN 978-1-914059-29-2)
16. *Dust of Glory The First Anglo-Afghan War 1839–1842, its Causes and Course* Bill Whitburn (ISBN 978-1-914059-33-9)
17. *Saarbruck to Sedan The Franco-German War 1870–1871 Volume 1* Ralph Weaver (ISBN 978-1-914059-88-9)
18. *The Battle of Lissa 1866 How the Industrial Revolution Changed the Face of Naval Warfare* Quintin Barry (ISBN 978-1-914059-92-6)
19. *The Zulu Kingdom and the Boer Invasion of 1837–1840* John Laband (ISBN 978-1-914059-89-6)
20. *The Fire of Venture Was in His Veins* Major Allan Wilson and the Shangani Patrol 1893 David Snape (ISBN 978-1-914059-90-2)
21. *From the Atacama to the Andes Battles of the War of the Pacific 1879–1883* Alan Curtis (ISBN 978-1-914059-90-2)
22. *The Rise of the Sikh Soldier The Sikh Warrior Through the Ages, c1700–1900* Gurinder Singh Mann (ISBN 978-1-915070-52-4)
23. *Victorian Crusaders British and Irish Volunteers in the Papal Army 1860–70* Nicholas Schofield (ISBN 978-1-915070-53-1)
24. *The Battle for the Swiepwald Austria's Fatal Blunder at Königgrätz, the climactic battle of the Austro-Prussian War, 3 July 1866* Ernst Heidrich (ISBN 978-1-915070-49-4)
25. *British Military Panoramas Battle in The Round, 1800–1914* Ian F.W. Beckett (ISBN 978-1-915113-84-9)
26. *Onwards to Omdurman The Anglo-Egyptian Campaign to Reconquer the Sudan, 1896–1898* Keith Surridge (ISBN 978-1-915070-51-7)
27. *Hungary 1849 The Summer Campaign* Wilhelm Ramming, Christopher Pringle (editor) (ISBN 978-1-915113-80-1)
28. *Line in the Sand French Foreign Legion Forts and Fortifications in Morocco 1900–1926* Richard Jeynes (ISBN 978-1-915113-83-2)
29. *The Republic Fights Back The Franco-German War 1870-1871 Volume 2* Ralph Weaver (ISBN 978-1-915070-50-0)
30. *Controlling the Frontier Southern Africa 1806–1828, The Cape Frontier Wars and The Fetcani Alarm* Hugh Driver (ISBN 978-1-915113-78-8)
31. *The Battle of Magersfontein Victory and defeat on the South African veld, 10–12 December 1899* Garth Benneyworth (ISBN 978-1-915113-79-5)
32. *Too Little Too Late The Campaign in West and South Germany June–July 1866* Michael Embree (ISBN 978-1-804513-77-4)
33. *The Destruction of the Imperial Army* Volume 1: The Opening Engagements of the Franco-German War 1870–71 Grenville Bird (ISBN 978-1-915113-81-8)
34. *Kitchener* The Man Not the Myth Anne Samson (ISBN 978-1-804513-84-2)
35. *From Ironclads to Dreadnoughts* The Development of the German Battleship, 1864–1918 Dirk Nottelmann & David M. Sullivan (ISBN 978-1-804511-84-8)
36. *The Destruction of the Imperial Army* Volume 2: The Battles around Metz Grenville Bird (ISBN 978-1-804511-85-5)
37. *More Work Than Glory* Buffalo Soldiers in the United States Army, 1866–1916 John P Langellier (ISBN 978-1-804513-34-7)
38. *The Spioenkop Campaign* The Battles to Relieve Ladysmith 17–27 January 1900 Robert Davidson (ISBN 978-1-804513-31-6)
39. *The Destruction of the Imperial Army* Volume 3: *The Sedan Campaign 1870* Grenville Bird (ISBN 978-1-804513-32-3)
40. *The Destruction of the Imperial Army* Volume 4: *Sedan, Strasbourg and Metz* 1870 Grenville Bird (ISBN 978-1-804514-59-7)
41. *Memorandum on the Prussian Army in Relation to the Campaign of 1866* Lieutenant Colonel W.E.M Reilly (ISBN 978-1-804516-27-0)
42. *Black Week: The British Army and Defeat in Anglo-Boer War 1899-1900* Quintin Barry (ISBN 978-1-804511-86-2)
43. *War in the East. A Military History of the Russo-Turkish War 1877-78* Quintin Barry (ISBN 978-1-804517-30-7)
44. *The First Schleswig-Holstein War 1848-50* Nick Svendsen (ISBN 978-1-804517-36-9)
45. *The Hundred Thousand Sons of St Louis* Ralph Weaver (ISBN 978-1-804517-37-6)
46. *Bismarck's First War: The Campaign in Schleswig and Jutland 1864* Michael Embree (ISBN 978-1-804517-38-3)
47. *The Honvéd War. Armies of the Hungarian War of Independence 1848-49* Nigel James Smith (ISBN 978-1-804514-60-3)
48. *Radestzky's Marches. The Campaigns of 1848 and 1849 in Upper Italy* Michael Embree (ISBN 978-1-804517-42-0)
49. *The Campaign on the Loire 1870-71: Orléans and Le Mans* Quintin Barry (ISBN 978-1-804517-82-6)
50. *The British Empire's Regulars 1880-1914: Soldiers of Britain, India and Africa* Wendell Scholander (ISBN 978-1-804515-62-4)
51. *The Last Throw of the Dice: Bourbaki and Werder in Eastern France 1870-71* Quintin Barry (ISBN 978-1-804517-78-9)
52. *Three Weeks in November. A Military History of the Swiss Civil War of 1847* Ralph Weaver (ISBN 978-1-804518-49-6)
53. *The Battle of Wörth August 6th 1870* Lieut.-Col. G.F.R. Henderson (ISBN 978-1-804517-90-1)
54. *The Battle of Spicheren August 6th 1870* Lieut.-Col. G.F.R. Henderson (ISBN 978-1-804518-50-2)
55. *The Serbian Army in the Wars for Independence against Turkey 1876-1878* Dusan M. Babac (ISBN 978-1-804518-69-4)
56. *The Campaign in Alsace August 1870* Brigadier-General J.P. Du Cane, C.B. (ISBN 978-1-804518-82-3)